Talking to God

What the Bible Teaches about Prayer

Thomas L. Constable

Foreword by Warren W. Wiersbe

Baker Books

A Division of Baker Book House Co
Grand Rapids, Michigan 49516

© 1995 by Thomas L. Constable

Published by Baker Books,
a division of Baker Book House Company
P.O. Box 6287
Grand Rapids, Michigan 49516-6287

Printed in the United States of America

Library of Congress Cataloging-in-Publication Data

Constable, Thomas L., 1939–
    Talking to God : what the Bible teaches about prayer / Thomas L. Constable ; foreword by Warren W. Wiersbe.
        p.   cm.
    Includes bibliographical references and indexes.
    ISBN 0-8010-2021-2 (pbk.)
    1. Prayer—Christianity. 2. Prayer—Biblical teaching. I. Title.
BV210.2.C65   1995
248.3'2—dc20   95-19658

Contents

Foreword

Samuel Johnson once told his friend and biographer James Boswell that "to reason philosophically on the nature of prayer was very unprofitable."

I agree with Johnson. Prayer isn't something you take into the laboratory and analyze scientifically, any more than you would analyze falling in love or the feeling you get when you hear beautiful music. But reasoning theologically about prayer is a different thing altogether, and that's where this book comes in.

We learn to pray by praying and by studying God's Word and by getting acquainted with the biblical masters of prayer. Thomas L. Constable brings together *from all of Scripture* the basic elements of effective praying and explains how those elements apply to believers and churches today. This survey of prayer in Scripture is one of the best I have ever seen, and I'm grateful for it.

Be sure to keep your Bible handy and look up the references the author cites. Dr. Constable wrote this book not to replace your Bible but to help you better understand your Bible.

The most important part of our Christian life is the part that only God sees. No believer rises any higher than his or her prayer life. I hope you take the message of this book seriously, because it can transform your life.

Warren W. Wiersbe
Author, conference speaker

Preface

All my life I have had questions about prayer. Thanks to the influence of godly parents, a good home church, and certain influential friends and teachers, prayer and Bible study have been two of my primary interests. When I was searching for a subject on which to write a doctoral dissertation at Dallas Theological Seminary, what the Bible teaches about prayer seemed an obvious choice. I wanted a subject that would keep me in the Scriptures and that would keep my interest. For more than a year I went through the Bible from Genesis to Revelation, studying all the references to prayer as I came to them. Then I read all the books on the subject that I thought would be helpful, and finally I wrote the dissertation. It proved tremendously profitable to me. I found that the Bible teaching on prayer is completely self-consistent. Even though I discovered that the answers to some of my questions are probably unknowable, due to the limits of God's revelation and my understanding, what God has revealed in the Bible about prayer makes sense.

This study did not satisfy my interest in the subject of prayer as I initially thought it would. Rather it fueled that interest. In the twenty-five years since I wrote my dissertation, I have continued to read books on prayer that have caught my attention. I have not attempted to read everything published on the subject. That would be impossible, and it would absorb the time of almost any person who attempted such a herculean task, since the volume of literature on prayer is overwhelming.

For more than twenty years I have also taught courses on prayer at Dallas Seminary. My students and I have studied what the Bible teaches on prayer, how saints through church history have prayed, and how prayer relates to the Christian life and to Christian ministry. Students have shown great interest in these courses, for which I am grateful to God and to them. Some of the most motivated students have been Doctor of Ministry students, people who have been in ministry for many years and who see the importance of prayer, who want to learn more about it, and who want to pray better. I do not consider myself a master of this subject or of the practice of prayer. However, I do believe that an understanding of what the Bible teaches about prayer not only will enable any person to pray better, but also will motivate him or her to pray more. That has been my experience and the experience of my fellow students of prayer.

There are many different approaches to prayer that writers on this subject have taken. This book seeks to stress what the Bible itself reveals about prayer. Thus it is a biblical theology of prayer, although the style is popular rather than academic. I hope that people who want to know what the Bible says about prayer will find this little volume helpful and stimulating.

Over the years many people have encouraged me to put this material in print. My wife, Mary, has long wished that many other people could profit from it. One former student and very close friend, the Reverend Terry Wood, gave me no rest until I submitted the manuscript for publication, and to Terry I owe a special debt of thanks. My desire is that God will use this small contribution to the already huge library of books on prayer to bring help to many people who have questions about prayer or problems with prayer, or who want to understand prayer better.

John 15:5

"I am the vine; you are the branches. If a man remains in me and I in him, he will bear much fruit; apart from me you can do nothing."

1

What Is Prayer Anyway?

Most people think of prayer as a way to contact God. Consequently, regardless of the religious label they attach to themselves, they pray more or less frequently. Instinctively people believe in God, and instinctively they pray to God. Christians, however, have a special interest in prayer. We believe it is a way to contact the true God who has revealed himself in love and who has spoken to us already in his Word, the Bible.

The volume of literature available on the subject of prayer testifies to the popularity of this practice. On the average, about two new books on prayer appear each month on the shelves of bookstores in America. Some of these are scientific studies that investigate prayer philosophically or psychologically. The largest group consists of devotional books that urge us to pray more. Comparatively few books, like this one, deal with the subject theologically. That is, they seek to set forth what the Bible teaches about prayer.

Prayers and references to prayer appear in sixty-two of the sixty-six books of the Bible; the exceptions are the Song

15

of Solomon, Obadiah, Haggai, and 2 John. Several Bible books give considerable attention to prayer: Genesis, Numbers, Judges, Matthew, Luke, Acts, 2 Corinthians, Ephesians, Philippians, Colossians, 1 and 2 Thessalonians, James, and 1 Peter. The Book of Psalms stands in a class by itself since it is a book of prayers. The Old Testament contains more information about prayer, and the New Testament stresses the importance of prayer. The two biblical characters who said the most about prayer were Jesus Christ and the apostle Paul.

The Bible presents God as a person who has communicated with us and who invites us to communicate with him. Since God is the sovereign Creator and we are finite creatures, we need to know what he has revealed about how we can and should communicate with him. The Christian's relationship to his or her heavenly Father is by definition the most important one that he or she enjoys. Therefore it is essential that we know how to communicate with God acceptably and effectively.

No verse in the Bible gives us a definition of prayer per se. Consequently we must discover what prayer is by examining the prayers and references to prayer in the Bible if we want a biblical definition. Prayer is talking to God. It is expressing our thoughts and feelings to deity.

In almost every prayer recorded or referred to in the Bible, the true God is the person addressed in prayer (2 Chron. 6:14; Eph. 3:14–15). In a few instances, a person prayed to a false god, an idol (Isa. 45:20). So the word *prayer* refers specifically to speech addressed to a being regarded as deity by the person praying. Moreover, the Bible limits prayer to human speech Godward. There is no indication in Scripture that animals pray to God. The biblical writers did not describe angelic speech to God as prayer, although it may be. Furthermore, the word always refers to our words to God and never to his words to us. The Bible does not use the term *prayer* to describe divine-human dialogue either. It uses it specifically to refer to our words to God. His words to us are something other than prayer: revelation, answer, response.

Several different Hebrew and Greek words, from the oldest Old and New Testament documents, translate as "prayer" in our English versions. They refer to general or specific types of speech directed to God. "Prayer" usually refers to any and every expression of our thoughts and feelings to God, audible or inaudible. The word specifically refers to petitions or requests of God (James 5:13–18). We find both uses of the word in Scripture.

From this brief introduction to prayer, we will move into a more detailed study of the different types of prayer that the Bible presents.

Psalm 51:1–10

Have mercy on me, O God,
　according to your unfailing love;
according to your great compassion
　blot out my transgressions.
Wash away all my iniquity
　and cleanse me from my sin.

For I know my transgressions,
　and my sin is always before me.
Against you, you only, have I sinned
　and done what is evil in your sight,
so that you are proved right when you speak
　and justified when you judge.
Surely I was sinful at birth,
　sinful from the time my mother conceived me.
Surely you desire truth in the inner parts;
　you teach me wisdom in the inmost place.

Cleanse me with hyssop, and I will be clean;
　wash me, and I will be whiter than snow.
Let me hear joy and gladness;
　let the bones you have crushed rejoice.
Hide your face from my sins
　and blot out all my iniquity.

Create in me a pure heart, O God,
　and renew a steadfast spirit within me.

2

A Prayer Tool Kit

My father was an avid do-it-yourselfer. Almost every Saturday he would work on some project around our house. Sometimes he would repair something that had broken or would build something new. I would often help him during my elementary and high-school years. We enjoyed working together. One of his do-it-yourself maxims was, "The right tool makes any job easier." As you can imagine, he had a lot of tools.

Prayers are similar to tools. They enable us to do work with God. Just as there are many different kinds of tools, so there are many varieties of prayers. Identifying the different spiritual tools that God has given us to work with is essential before we can select the right one and use it to serve a particular function. In this chapter we want to look into God's toolbox, the Bible, to observe and examine the various kinds of prayer.

We can divide all prayers into two groups: prayers in which we ask God for something and those in which we tell him something. As human beings our spoken communication is divisible into these two aspects as well. We ask questions, and we make affirmations. Some people have inquisitive minds. They want to know what makes things tick. Children, for example, often wear us out with their endless whys. Other people ask fewer questions. Their side of a conversation tends to consist of statements rather than questions.

As we have noted in the preceding chapter, prayer is the label that the Bible puts on our communication with God. We ask God things, and we tell him things. Our prayers are our verbal tools that we use to get things done with God.

Questioning God

According to the Bible, God is a person who has infinite knowledge and wisdom. He knows how everything began and how it will end. He knows what works best in human life, and he wants people to experience what is best. It is natural, therefore, that we should ask God questions. This is precisely what we find happening in the selective record of human history that the Bible contains.

In the Bible we read of people asking God for information on a variety of subjects, a variety as wide as their interests. For example, David asked God why the nations were in turmoil (Ps. 2:1, Acts 4:25). Joshua asked God why he had brought the Israelites across the Jordan River miraculously, only to allow them to fall before their enemies (Josh. 7:7–9). David often asked God if he should take a particular course of military action (e.g., 2 Sam. 2:1). Job pleaded with God to identify his sin, sin that he himself could not identify (Job 7:11–21). One of the psalmists wanted to know why God would not respond to his prayers when everything around him seemed to be falling apart (Ps. 10:1–2). The apostle Paul asked God about the identity of the person who appeared to him on the Damascus Road (Acts 9:5).

We can learn what to expect when we ask God for information by noting how God responded to questions in prayer. Interestingly, God often answered these prayers by giving special revelation. In the early history of humankind, God revealed himself through visions, dreams, and in direct encounters (Num. 12:6–8). He often communicated answers to people's questions directly to the individuals who prayed. As history unfolded and people had the benefit of divine revelation that stood written in black on white, his direct answers to questions voiced in prayer became increasingly uncommon. He had previously answered them. Frequently the answers to the questions that we pray today stand revealed in Scripture already. We do not need new answers, but instead need to find the answers that God has already given. This is especially true when we want information about God's major plans and purposes, why important things are happening as they are, and how things are going to turn out ultimately.

When we want information that will affect specific choices that we must make, God has also revealed how to obtain those answers. He has told us to make those decisions in dependence on himself and primarily by applying the wise precepts and the examples that he has recorded for us in the Bible (Prov. 3:5–6). The Holy Spirit enables us to make wise choices when we seek to live in the light of what God has revealed. When our forefathers lacked the full revelation that we enjoy in Scripture, an audible voice giving guidance was necessary. Today the Holy Spirit guides disciples of Jesus into the truth primarily by illuminating the truth that God has given us in Scripture (John 14:23–26).

In the history of God's dealings with humanity that Scripture records, the clarity of God's guidance was propor-

tionate to the importance of the decision the person praying faced. For example, God's directions to Adam and Eve
about their responsibilities as the ancestors of the human
race were crystal clear to them (Gen. 1:28–30; 2:16–17).
His instructions to righteous Noah were unmistakable
because they would affect all of mankind from then on (e.g.,
Gen. 6:13–21; 7:1–4). His promises to Abraham about his
using that patriarch and his descendants to be a special channel of blessing for all humanity were likewise obvious (Gen.
12:1–3, 7; 15). When Abraham's servant went back to Pad-
dan-aram, the old country, to secure a bride for his master's
son, God's guidance to Rebekah was clear. It would be
through Isaac and his wife that God would fulfill those
promises.

By contrast, today God may not grant every young man
seeking his will concerning a life partner such clear guidance. It would not be wise for a young man wanting God's
guidance in choosing a mate to ask God to lead the woman
of God's choice to offer to fill his gas tank. Rebekah offered
to water the servant's camels, but that marriage had special
significance in view of God's stated plans. The consequences of a mate choice for most people today, although
those consequences are certainly important, may not be as
significant as was the choice of a wife for Abraham's heir.
The more important a decision is, from God's viewpoint,
the more definite his guidance is. Sincere Christians want
to please God in all their decisions, but not all our decisions
are equally important. Therefore, God gives us no special
guidance in the multitude of small decisions that we make
daily, such as which socks to wear today. These decisions
are up to us.

By observing God's responses to prayers of inquiry in the
Bible, we learn that God never rebukes the sincere questions
of believers when they struggle to trust him. God is patient

with people who have questions and who bring their problems to him for help. He also gave specific answers to specific questions in many cases, not unsatisfying and frustrating general answers. He treats people's prayers of inquiry seriously even when they do not articulate very serious problems. He does not brush us off.

However, God may not answer immediately or as soon as we might want (Job 7:11–12). Moreover sometimes no answer is his answer. God has already given the answers to some of our inquiries, and we can find those answers by searching the Scriptures (John 5:39a).

Asking for Ourselves

Some sincere Christians believe that it is selfish and not very trusting to ask God to give us anything. Some Christians believe that praying for personal needs is more a mark of unbelief than of trust in God. After all, since God loves us perfectly, will he not do what is best for us?

Such an attitude may superficially sound spiritual. However, it contradicts Jesus' clear teaching that God's children should ask him for their needs (Matt. 6:9–13; Luke 11:1–4). It also ignores James's statement that we do not have some things from God because we do not ask him for them (James 4:2). God not only encourages us to ask him for what we need, but also commands us to do so. He does so to teach us to look to him for our needs because he is our provider.

God's responses to personal petitions teach us what we can expect when we pray this way. Sometimes God granted a request, but sometimes he did not. Sometimes he waited to give an answer. We shall investigate the conditions we need to meet for securing favorable answers to our prayers in a later chapter. For now, appreciate that often God graciously gives what we request for ourselves.

Jesus told his disciples the parable of the persistent friend to help them realize that God will always give what is best to his children who ask him in prayer (Luke 11:5–13). A friend may eventually give his neighbor what he needs because he is his friend. However, God is our Father, and a good father always gives his children what is best for them at the best time. Therefore we should keep on asking in prayer, keep on seeking God's face, and keep on knocking on heaven's door.

God does not grant every one of our requests just because we ask. Sometimes we make foolish petitions. Moses once asked God to kill him because he felt discouraged (Num. 11:15). God understands our situation and gives us what is best. Sometimes when old people pray for longer life God takes them home to heaven. If he does, that is best for them then.

Asking for Others

Intercessory prayer is prayer that we offer for someone other than ourselves. We act as a priest and stand between God and another person, seeking to influence God with our words when we intercede in prayer.

We can pray one of two things for another person. We can ask God to bless that person or to curse him or her. Jesus taught his disciples to bless their enemies (Matt. 5:44). Paul taught us to pray for all the saints (Eph. 6:18; cf. James 5:16) and for all people, specifically for governmental rulers (1 Tim. 2:1–2). God wants us to ask him to bring blessing on everyone. He will not do this as much if we refrain from interceding (James 4:2).

In view of Jesus' and Paul's teaching that we should bless our enemies (Luke 6:27–28; Rom. 12:14), how can we understand instances of people in the Bible praying that

God would curse others? These are the imprecatory prayers that appear mainly in the Old Testament (e.g., Num. 10:35; Judg. 5:31; Ps. 28:3–5; Jer. 11:20). Should Jesus' followers not emulate his example as he hung on the cross and prayed for his Father to forgive those who crucified him (Luke 23:34; cf. Acts 7:60)? Should we follow the example of the Old Testament saints or of Jesus?

Several factors are helpful to remember as we consider the problem of imprecatory prayer. First, we need to note that under the Mosaic economy one of God's primary purposes was to demonstrate his holiness and justice (Ps. 79:10–13; Ezek. 28:22). Consequently it was appropriate for Old Testament saints to ask God to do this by judging sinners immediately (Ps. 144:5–8). God ordained holy war when the Israelites entered the Promised Land to judge sin in the Canaanites who then occupied the land (Deut. 7:24–25; Isa. 26:15). It was God's will for the Israelites to occupy that land then. It was therefore appropriate for them to ask him to destroy their enemies (Exod. 14:25–31; Dan. 5:20). God's purpose is different in the present age. Now he is demonstrating his love and grace primarily (John 1:17). Therefore typical prayers in the New Testament call on God to show mercy to sinners and to save them (Acts 7:60; Rom. 10:1; cf. 2 Pet. 3:9). "Not until the supreme exhibition of God's displeasure at sin, demonstrated by the death of His Son upon the cross, was it possible for the believer to wait patiently while God's longsuffering permitted the wicked to enjoy his temporary success. Nor was the longsuffering of God properly understood until Jesus came to earth to teach His love to men" (Gleason L. Archer Jr., *Survey of Old Testament Introduction*, rev. ed. [Chicago: Moody, 1974], 453).

Remember too that God inspired some of the imprecations that stand recorded in Scripture. God inspired all

Scripture (2 Tim. 3:16), but he did not inspire all the deeds that the biblical writers recorded: lies, murders, and other sins. Some of the imprecations in the Psalms, for example, were part of the prayers that God inspired the psalmists to pray and to record. This does not mean that their imprecations are models that we should reproduce. They were God's will and appropriate for the psalmists to pray then, but his will for us now is different.

The motive of the person praying was significant in biblical imprecatory prayers. The appropriate ones did not arise out of a spirit of personal vengefulness. Rather, hatred of sin and a desire for God's glory usually moved Old Testament saints to pray this way (Ps. 5:10–11; 21:10–12; 139:19–22; cf. 2 Sam. 1:19–27).

Some of the imprecatory prayers in the Bible were prophecies (Ps. 137:8–9; cf. Isa. 13; 15). They were God-given predictions of what he would do expressed in prayer. Sometimes there were conditions understood, if not stated, allowing for a change if the people repented.

We also need to remember that in the ancient Near East the language of expression tended to be more intense, emphatic, and emotional than it is in the modern West. Hyperbole was quite common. To modern western ears these expressions of strong feeling seem even stronger than they did to ancient eastern ears.

As history unfolded and as revelation progressed, God revealed more and more about how he would punish the wicked and balance the scales of justice. We can know more about this by reading our Bibles than Job or David could have known, for example. Consequently we should feel less anxiety about God vindicating himself by punishing the wicked than did those who called on God to do that in ancient times. To put the problem in perspective, we need to remember that even in the Old Testament we have relatively few prayers of imprecation. Only about sixty-five verses contain them.

I have not found any examples of true imprecatory prayers in the New Testament books dealing with the church age. Some expressions that may appear to be imprecatory prayers are really pious wishes (1 Cor. 16:22; Gal. 1:8–9; 5:12; 2 Tim. 4:14). Prayers are statements addressed to God, but pious wishes are statements addressed to no one in particular. During the future tribulation period that is coming on the earth, believers who have died as martyrs will call on God to avenge them (Rev. 6:9–10). These prayers are not exactly the same as the prayers of saints alive on the earth. They are, therefore, not examples of imprecations in the usual sense of that term.

Returning to the general subject of intercession, we must point out that these prayers have moved God to act in remarkable ways according to the biblical record. When Moses interceded for the Israelites in their battle with the Amalekites, God's people prevailed over their enemies (Exod. 17:11). Moses' intercession moved God to be merciful to the Israelites after they had apostatized and built the golden calf (Exod. 32:10–14) and when they rebelled at Kadesh Barnea (Num. 14:13–20). Moses was a model intercessor and a great example of a faithful leader. His outstanding ministry included frequent prayer for those under his authority. Samuel was also a notable intercessor (1 Sam. 7:9–10; 12:17–23; cf. Jer. 15:1).

The historical and prophetical books of the Old Testament contain many examples of intercessory prayers. Of course, the Psalter is full of intercession. Paul's writings also abound with intercessory prayers, as do the other New Testament epistles, although Paul's prayers are more numerous than those of the other New Testament writers.

Jesus Christ's present ministry is mainly intercessory. He prays from heaven for believers (Rom. 8:34; Heb. 7:25). Theologically, Jesus' intercessory ministry involves his praying to keep us from falling before temptation and failing because of weakness. As our advocate, he pleads our case with the Father after we sin (1 John 2:1). Nevertheless both types of praying involve intercession. The Holy Spirit also intercedes for Christians (Rom. 8:26–27). He articulates our deepest feelings to the Father when we struggle to express ourselves. Even when we cannot express how we feel, the Holy Spirit knows and translates those feelings into prayers that the Father understands. The members of the Trinity do not pray to each other in the manner in which we pray to God. Nonetheless the Son and the Spirit intercede for us with the Father.

The answers to intercessory prayers that God has recorded in his Word indicate that we can move God to effect some changes in people and in circumstances through prayer. These changes are real; they are objective rather than simply changes that he makes in us as we pray. The fact that Jesus is interceding for his own now should help us to appreciate that intercession can be effective. Moreover, God commands us to intercede for others (1 Tim. 2:1–4).

Conversing with God

When people pray, they frequently enter into simple conversation with God. I do not mean that God responds to them audibly or that God's response is part of prayer. As we noted (chap. 1), prayer as the Bible uses that term describes only our words to God, not his response to us. By simple conversation I mean to exclude the specific subjects of prayer that the writers of Scripture have designated with special words: confession, complaint, praise, and thanksgiving. We are now moving into the second basic type of prayer, namely, prayers in which we tell God something rather than ask him for something. Let's consider this general narrative prayer, the kind in which we tell God something in a conversational way.

In normal, interpersonal communication we sometimes initiate a conversation or make an unsolicited statement. At other times we respond verbally to someone else's initiative by making a reply or a response. We find examples of both kinds of narrative prayer in the Bible.

Throughout history, as the Bible records it, people laid certain facts before the Lord in prayer as a servant would explain a situation to his or her master (1 Sam. 8:21; Ezek. 20:49). Prayers of this type frequently arose out of feelings of fear (1 Sam. 16:2; Acts 9:13–14) or pain (Job 7:11–21). People who prayed this way wanted to let God know how they were feeling. Of course, God always knows exactly how we feel about our situation in life because he knows all things and has compassion for every human being. Nevertheless, verbalizing these feelings to God in prayer gives us a measure of relief (Phil. 4:6–7).

Sometimes when I come home from work I want to tell Mary, my wife, that I feel good or bad even though she can often sense this. Yet articulating my feelings helps me, and it gives both of us a sense that we are sharing life as partners. It improves my feelings, and it strengthens our fellowship. Of course, she does the same. This is also the effect of our pouring our hearts out to God, our closest friend, partner, and Father.

At other times something that God has said or done elicits a response from us in prayer. Praise and thanksgiving are two specific responses that we will consider later. Here we want to focus on prayer responses to something that God has said in his Word.

Biblical personalities whose lives stand recorded in Scripture often told God that they had heard him (1 Sam. 3:4; Acts 9:10). These are normal conversational reactions to the speech of someone who is addressing us. After a friend has told us something, we may respond, "I see what you mean," or "I hear you." This response is considerate conversation. It results in good rapport between the people talking. Similarly our verbal acknowledgment that we have heard and understood what God has said to us through his Word creates a sense of good fellowship (see 1 Sam. 3:9). In the Bible prayers of inquiry or petition frequently follow prayers of response (e.g., Isa. 6:8–9). The pattern is common in all interpersonal communication.

Report prayers appear in the biographical sections of Scripture, and they help us to appreciate a biblical character's interaction with God. Response prayers normally follow instances in which God revealed himself to individuals or groups of people.

God presents himself in the Bible as being open and interested in hearing whatever concerns his children (James 5:13; 1 Pet. 5:7). He wants to hear whatever interests us, even the smallest, most insignificant details of our lives. Consequently we should feel free to unburden our hearts and tell God anything and everything. He is the friend who sticks closer than a brother. We can converse with him casually and comfortably as we would with our most intimate acquaintance.

Even though God already knows whatever we might tell him before we tell him, he still wants us to tell him. This proves that God desires fellowship with us. Fellowship with God is one of the primary purposes of prayer. Family members who do not talk to each other enough develop problems in their relationship. Keeping the lines of communication open with God is also essential to a healthy spiritual relationship. In marriage communication is usually informal and unrehearsed, and it can be that way with our heavenly bridegroom too.

There is definitely a subjective value to prayer. Verbalizing our thoughts and feelings gives us a sense of relief (Phil. 4:6–7). Discussing a particular situation with a friend affords this satisfaction between human beings. Prayer of this type can be similar to having a conversation with someone you love.

Confessing Sins

One kind of narrative prayer that the Bible refers to frequently is confession. A prayer of confession is one in which we acknowledge to God that what we have done is contrary to his will. We admit to God that we have sinned.

God does not expect us to identify and to confess every sin of which we may be guilty. That would be impossible, for we are aware of only some of our sins. John Calvin reportedly said that no one knows the hundredth part of the sin that clings unto his soul. We commit sins of omission as well as sins of commission; we fail to do things that we should do as well as do things that we should not do (James 4:17). We sin in our thoughts as well as in our actions. Jesus taught that God regards a lustful look and an adulterous act as equally contrary to his will (Matt. 5:28). Unjustified anger is just as sinful as murder (Matt. 5:22). The consequences are different, but the acts are both sinful. We sin with our tongues as well as with our hands and feet (Matt. 5:22). Even failure to love God and our fellow man perfectly constitutes sin (Matt. 5:44–48). Sometimes we rationalize a situation without being consciously aware that we

are distorting the truth. I'm speaking about Christians as
well as non-Christians (1 John 1:6–10). God does ask us,
however, to confess any and every sin of which we are
aware. He promises that when we do so he will cleanse us
from the defilement of all our sins, not just those that we
are aware of and confess (1 John 1:9).

Jesus instructed his disciples to ask God to forgive their
sins (Matt. 6:12; Luke 11:4). However, Paul taught that
when a person trusts in Jesus Christ as Savior, God forgives
all his or her sins—past, present, and future (Rom. 8:1; cf.
Rom. 5:1). How can we reconcile these two apparently con-
flicting revelations concerning our forgiveness?

The Bible speaks about two kinds of forgiveness. There
is the legal or forensic forgiveness that we experience when
we become Christians. When we trust in Jesus Christ for
our salvation, God promises never to condemn us for our
sins (Rom. 8:1). He will never reject us. His Son paid the
penalty for our sins (2 Cor. 5:21; 1 Pet. 2:24); consequently,
we will never have to pay that penalty.

The new birth brings us into a new relationship with God.
We become his children and enter his spiritual family. As
saved sons of God, we continue to sin because we still have
a sinful human nature, we live in a sinful world, and Satan
tempts us. Our sinning does not result in God disinheriting
us, but it does result in our displeasing him. In a human
family a child breaks fellowship within the family when he
disobeys his parents, but his father does not throw him out
of the family. Likewise we do not lose our salvation when
we sin (John 10:28–29), but our fellowship with our Father
suffers. Confession restores fellowship on both levels, the
human and the divine.

Suppose a judge had a teenage son who broke the law
by speeding. The son comes before the judge and receives
a guilty verdict and a fine. Because the judge is the young

man's loving father he decides to pay his son's fine for him. This makes the son legally free and under no further obligation to the state. However, when the son goes home that night he discovers that his dad has decided to ground him for a month for speeding. The legal responsibility had been met, but there were still obligations within the family that the son had to fulfill because of his act. Jesus Christ paid the legal obligation we owe God because of our sin, but we also have an obligation to the Father as members of his family. However, God graciously does not ask us to do anything more than confess our sins to make things right with him.

What does confession involve? The Greek word in the New Testament that translators have rendered "confess" (*homologeo*) means "to say the same thing," to acknowledge that what we have done is truly sinful. Some Christians find it impossible to believe that that is all that God requires, even though the meaning of the Greek word is beyond dispute. They have added that there must be evidence of a change of behavior, too, or the confession is not genuine. However, that is not what God says in his Word. He says that all we need to do is to acknowledge that what we have done or not done is a sin against God, to say the same thing about our sin that God says. Calling sin something else makes God a liar (1 John 1:10). This is an extremely serious thing to do. Confessing does not mean just pasting a label on our sin, however. To say the same thing about our sin as God does involves assuming his attitude toward it too. Changing our attitude is what the Bible calls repenting. A changed attitude should result in changed behavior.

The way other people have dealt with us in the past, however, colors our understanding of how God deals with us. Many people cannot accept God's gracious forgiveness because they have never or rarely experienced that kind of treatment at the hands of other people. That is why it is so important that we believe what God has said in his Word. Obtaining forgiveness for confessing without doing penance of some kind seems too good to be true to some Christians, but God says it is true. All we have to do to experience restoration of our fellowship with God is to take the same view of our sin as God does. When we do that, our Father will forgive us those sins, and he will cleanse us from all our unrighteousness, even the sins of which we are unaware.

Just as children prefer to cover up their mistakes, so we all hate to admit that we have done wrong. One of the ways that we try to cover up is to disguise our sins. Dr. Lewis Sperry Chafer was walking down a street in Dallas, Texas, one day with a man who believed in sinless perfection (that once a person becomes a Christian he stops sinning). The gentleman was claiming to Dr. Chafer that he had not sinned since he had entered God's family. Suddenly a gust of wind caught his hat and blew it down the sidewalk. The perfectionist's immediate reaction was to use the Lord's name in vain. When he had recovered his hat, Dr. Chafer said to him, "I thought you told me that you had not sinned since you became a Christian. What do you call using the Lord's name in vain?" "Oh, that wasn't a sin," his companion responded. "That was just a mistake."

One common way that we avoid confessing—viewing sin as God views it—is to call it something else: a mistake, or a white lie, or a blunder. When we do that, we deceive ourselves, not God, and the truth is not in us (1 John 1:8). God calls sin *sin*. Children who refuse to admit that what they have done is disobedience do not enjoy restoration to family fellowship. When we say the same thing about our sin as God does, we are acknowledging that we have offended a holy God and are worthy of his wrath (Ps. 51:3–4; Jer. 3:13). When we rationalize our condition or behavior by giving it another name when it is really sin, we are not confessing but covering up. On the one hand, obtaining forgiveness is very easy, but on the other hand it is painfully difficult. It involves humbling ourselves, and that is never easy for proud human beings such as ourselves.

In the Bible there are many examples of individuals confessing their sins to God. (e.g., Ps. 66:18). There are also several instances of groups of people doing this corporately (Lev. 16:12, 31; Heb. 5:1, 3; 8:3). Great spiritual leaders of the past spoke for their contemporaries and confessed the sins of their people to God. Outstanding among these were Moses, David, Ezra, Nehemiah, Jeremiah, and Daniel.

The apostle James wrote that we should confess our faults to one another (James 5:16). In view of the context, the faults he seems to have had in mind were offenses against other people that spoil interpersonal relationships and make worship together difficult, if not impossible. We should acknowledge our sins against other people, not only to God but also to those individuals whom we have sinned against (Matt. 5:23–24). Failure to forgive others who have sinned against us will result in God not forgiving us (Matt. 6:14–15).

We can understand how this works when we think of healthy human family relations. If two children in a normal family have a fight, it affects their relationship with their parents as well as their relationship with each other. Their parents will not be content until the children confess and forgive each other. Child-to-child forgiveness is necessary before parent-to-child forgiveness can take place. Our horizontal relationships have to be right before our vertical relationship can be right.

Confession that God approved in the Bible was sometimes public (Acts 19:18–19). How should we handle public confession? The Bible does not give specific instructions, but biblical examples and common sense provide some guidance. It is wise to limit the circle of confession to those whom the offense has affected. There is no value in publicly confessing a sin in the hearing of those who have had no part in it or who are unaffected by it. Doing so sometimes does more harm than good. The Christian man who confesses in a church meeting that he has been secretly lusting after his neighbor's wife is going beyond what God requires. Since the sin was in his heart and only God knew about it, he should confess it only to God. The Christian woman who confesses publicly that she has cheated on her husband also has gone too far. She need only confess her sin to God, her husband, and the other man, assuming they were the only people affected by the sin. The pastor who confesses that he has been embezzling funds from the church treasury should confess his sin to his congregation as well as to God since he has sinned against all of them. But there is no reason he should take out an ad in his local newspaper to announce his sin. Publicizing sin beyond the circle of those affected brings reproach on the church and the Lord.

How can we become more sensitive to sin in our lives so we can confess when we need to? It is interesting that some revelation from God or some greater insight into God's character usually triggered the instances of confession that God recorded in the Bible (Job 40:4–5). When we get to know God better and gain a deeper appreciation for his holiness, our own lives look sinful in comparison. This perspective produces conviction and confession (Isa. 6:5).

Confessing our sins is one way that we praise God. We glorify him by acknowledging that we have fallen short of his perfection (Josh. 7:19; Ezra 10:11). This constitutes testimony that he is holy. There are many examples of confessional prayer in the Bible. The Bible books in which records of apostasy abound are especially full of prayers of confession. The historical and prophetical books of the Old Testament record many such prayers in the life of ancient Israel.

The prayers of confession in Scripture teach us the great breadth of God's grace. He pardons every sin that his people confess, and he cleanses from all unrighteousness. Many people suffer under feelings of true guilt that they could remove if they would only confess their sins and believe God's promises of forgiveness (e.g., 1 John 1:9). Some extremely sensitive Christians suffer under feelings of false guilt; they are not really guilty before God, but they think they are. These dear people do not need to confess, but they do need to believe God's promises of forgiveness and to learn what is and what is not sin.

Even though God removes the guilt of our sins when we confess them, he does not usually remove all their consequences. David is a typical example. God forgave him for committing adultery with Bathsheba and for murdering her husband Uriah. David did not die immediately. Nevertheless many bad consequences followed those sins. The child that Bathsheba conceived died, and adultery and murder plagued David's family from then on. We should never conclude that because we can obtain forgiveness from God by confessing, it is all right to sin. Consequences will inevitably follow sin (Rom. 6:23). The man or woman who thinks, "I will be unfaithful to my mate and then confess my sin and receive forgiveness," is not really taking the same view of sin as God does. Such a person should not expect forgiveness and should expect consequences to follow that are God's punishment for deliberate sin.

Praising the Lord

We speak about praising and thanking God as almost syn-onymous terms in popular English conversation. The Bible, however, uses these words more specifically. Praise usually refers to our positive responses to the revelation of God's per-son that he has given in nature and in Scripture. Thanksgiv-ing typically describes our positive reaction to God's works.

The Book of Psalms contains more prayers of praise than does any other portion of Scripture, though prayers of praise are common throughout God's Word. The Israelites fre-quently praised God in public worship (e.g., 2 Chron. 29:28–30) as well as privately. Expressions of praise to God are common in Acts, the Epistles, and Revelation.

The more we know about God and the better we know him personally the more mature our praise will be. Chil-dren often reflect their concept of God by the way they pray. Recently a four-year-old friend of mine prayed that God would keep a police officer who attends our church safe. This boy has learned to appreciate God as a strong defender who is able to protect the vulnerable. As adults we too betray our understanding of God by how we praise him. One way to grow in our appreciation of the greatness of God's person is to look for his personal characteristics as we read his Word. These come through in direct teaching about God, but they are also obvious in his actions as he has revealed these through history and in our own experi-ence. The most majestic and glorious praise of God occurs in the Book of Revelation, in which saints who will be in God's presence in the future praise him for who he has proved himself to be throughout history. The particular aspects of God's character for which people praised him in Scripture include his goodness, his loyal love or lov-ingkindness, his faithfulness to his promises, his power, his eternality, his holiness, his wisdom, his truthfulness, his omnipresence, and his compassion.

When we contemplate God, our normal reaction will be to praise him. Lack of praise in our praying may indicate a lack of appreciation for his person or a shallow understanding of his character. If we want to cultivate our praise of God, we should get to know him better and review his characteristics that we already appreciate. Sometimes, as I drive to work, I do this by identifying characteristics of God that begin with succeeding letters of the alphabet, from A to Z.

It is very important that we get our information about God from his self-revelation in Scripture (2 Tim. 3:16; 2 Pet. 1:21). We tend to make God in our own image, as did the Greeks, who viewed their gods as human beings blown into superhuman proportions, warts and all. We could never imagine that the true God is the type of person that he has revealed himself to be if we sat down to figure out on our own what God is like. This is one reason that God has glorified his Word above his name (Ps. 138:2). (In ancient Near Eastern thought, the name represented everything about the person who bore it. It was roughly equivalent to that person's reputation. Therefore when we read that the name of God was the focus of praise, it was the person of God as he has revealed himself that is the object of that praise.) His Word contains an articulate and extensive revelation of his person.

Giving Thanks in Everything

In praise we focus on God's person, but in thanksgiving we express a positive reaction to what God has done, his works. Prayers of thanksgiving express gratitude to God for favors, benefits, and mercies that he provides. Notwithstanding this fact, in biblical prayers of thanksgiving God himself, not just his blessings, is primary in the mind of the person praying. What he has done or given is the focus of the prayer, but the giver is more important than the gift.

Another biblical term that means the same thing as thanking God is "blessing" him (Deut. 8:10; 1 Chron. 29:10–19; Matt. 26:26–27; John 6:11). In prayers that bless God, the person praying thanks him for something that he has done. This is a different use of the word *bless* than what occurs when in intercessory prayer we ask God to bless someone. Then we mean that we want God to deal with the objects of our concern in a positive way, to pour out his goodness on them. When God is the person we bless in prayer, we are saying that we praise God as a response to some goodness that he has granted.

There are few prayers of thanksgiving in the Pentateuch and the prophetic books of the Old Testament. There are many, however, in the other historical books and the Psalms. The Pauline epistles abound with them. Paul typically thanked God for the people to whom he addressed his epistles, and then he prayed that God would give them something (e.g., Phil. 1:3–11). Paul often thanked God for the spiritual vitality of the people to whom he wrote (Rom. 1:8; 2 Cor. 8:11–16; Eph. 1:15–16; Col. 1:3–8; 1 Thess. 1:2–3). As is true of prayers of praise, throughout history prayers of thanksgiving increased in both number and fullness of expression with God's progressive self-revelation. As people became increasingly aware of God's great acts for them, they praised God more. Thanksgiving burst into full flower following the resurrection of Jesus Christ (1 Cor. 15:57). That great victory proves to all people that Jesus Christ's sacrifice fully satisfied God's demands against sinful humanity.

Probably the two greatest themes of thanksgiving are creation (Rev. 4) and redemption (Rev. 5). All of God's activities, however, have furnished the raw materials out of which people have fashioned their prayers of thanksgiving (Gen. 24:26–27; 2 Sam. 22:29–46; Ps. 9:3–6; 116; 118; Acts 28:15; 1 Cor. 1:4–9; 2 Cor. 4:15; Eph. 1:3–14; 1 Tim. 4:4–5; 1 Pet. 1:3–12). Both physical and spiritual provisions are the subjects of thanksgiving prayers, the former being more common in the Old Testament and the latter more common in the New.

Thanksgiving glorifies God (Ps. 50:23; Luke 17:11–19; Rom. 1:21). Therefore we should express our gratitude to God in prayer. Furthermore God has commanded Christians to thank him always (Col. 3:15–16; 4:2–4; Heb. 13:15) in every circumstance (Phil. 4:6–7; 1 Thess. 5:16–18) and for all things (Eph. 5:20). We can do this sincerely because God causes all things to work together for good for those who love him (Rom. 8:28). Thanksgiving is also a mark of spiritual vitality (Col. 2:6–7), whereas the absence of thanksgiving indicates a spiritual deficiency.

Complaining to God

Prayers of praise and thanksgiving express positive reactions to God's person and performance. There are also quite a few prayers in Scripture that express negative reactions to him. Biblical prayers of complaint usually accused God or blamed him because of some situation that the person praying regarded as bad (Exod. 5:22–23; Job 10:3–6; Ps. 42:9–10; Jer. 4:10). Sometimes the complaint sounds more like self-pity than accusation (1 Kings 19:14). Nevertheless these were prayers to God, not soliloquies.

Many of God's choice servants—Moses, Elijah, Job, David, Jeremiah, and Jonah—complained to him in prayer.

Frustration, discouragement, loneliness, worries, anger, and impatience caused them to complain. How did God respond when our spiritual forefathers complained to him? His responses are illuminating and encouraging. Characteristically he reacted with patient understanding. He understands when suffering saints chafe. He understands our true feelings even better than we do (Rom. 8:26). He does not punish us when we speak rashly because we feel uncomfortable. He treats us tenderly, as a loving and understanding father treats his distressed and unhappy children.

We can learn how to get through an uncomfortable situation that provokes complaints by noting the testimonies of biblical characters who finally emerged from their slough of despond. We need to keep God in view rather than turning from him in such situations. Job maintained his sanity during his monumental trials by talking to God and about God. He kept turning back to God rather than away from him. David said that when he went into the Lord's presence the hatred that he felt in his heart melted away (Ps. 73:3–17).

Many people tend to turn away from God when they experience discomfort. This is exactly the opposite reaction to the one that provided healing for many of God's people. Rather than dropping out of church we need to go there when we feel bad. Rather than stopping praying because we feel we should not complain to God we should honestly tell him how we feel. God's reactions to prayers of complaint in Scripture encourage us to believe that we never need fear telling God whatever is on our hearts. God is not looking for an opportunity to punish us. He desires to bless us. Being honest with God in prayer is the fastest and best way to begin to deal with our disappointments. If we cover them up or deny them, God has to discipline us first to get us back into fellowship with himself. However, if we are open with him, he needs only to deal with our handling of whatever situation has caused us to complain.

As we have seen in this chapter, prayer is a relational exercise. We communicate with another Person in prayer. I believe that God created the family with its interrelationships at least partially to help us understand our relationship with himself. Jesus revealed that God relates to his disciples as a good father relates to his children (Matt. 6:9; Luke 11:2). We can learn much about what God wants and how he will respond as we think about the ideal father. Scriptural revelation promotes this analogy. We can ask God for information and ask him to give us and others the things that we need and want. We can tell him whatever is on our minds. We can and should confess our sins to him. We should praise him for his matchless character and thank him for his gracious conduct. We can even complain to him knowing that he will understand and at the proper time heal our hurts.

1 Kings 8:23–30

"O LORD, God of Israel, there is no God like you in heaven above or on earth below—you who keep your covenant of love with your servants who continue wholeheartedly in your way. You have kept your promise to your servant David my father; with your mouth you have promised and with your hand you have fulfilled it—as it is today.

"Now LORD, God of Israel, keep for your servant David my father the promises you made to him when you said, 'You shall never fail to have a man to sit before me on the throne of Israel, if only your sons are careful in all they do to walk before me as you have done.' And now, O God of Israel, let your word that you promised your servant David my father come true.

"But will God really dwell on earth? The heavens, even the highest heaven, cannot contain you. How much less this temple I have built! Yet give attention to your servant's prayer and his plea for mercy, O LORD my God. Hear the cry and the prayer that your servant is praying in your presence this day. May your eyes be open toward this temple night and day, this place of which you said, 'My Name shall be there,' so that you will hear the prayer your servant prays toward this place. Hear the supplication of your servant and of your people Israel when they pray toward this place. Hear from heaven, your dwelling place, and when you hear, forgive."

3

Fitting Prayer into Daily Life

Jessica began collecting postage stamps as a hobby. Her parents had given her a modest stamp album, and she had accumulated several dozen stamps. One afternoon she sat down with her stamps and her album, intending to put her treasures neatly in their appropriate places. Immediately she realized that to get them organized and to put them in their proper spots she needed to look carefully at the stamps to distinguish them from each other. She had a particular interest in United States stamps. So the first thing she had to do was to separate U. S. stamps from the others and from the many different types of stickers that also filled the shoe box that was their temporary home. To her surprise she discovered that some stamps looked very much like U. S. stamps but were not. She also discovered that bits of envelopes stuck to some of the stamps, and she had to remove them carefully. In some cases the cancellation marks almost obliterated the stamp itself. She had to use a magnifying glass to determine what the stamp looked like before the post office cancelled it so she could position it in her album.

In studying what the Bible teaches about prayer, it is also important to distinguish prayer from other religious practices. Some of these practices appear to be prayer but are not. They resemble the ordinary stickers that look like postage stamps but are not. Other spiritual practices go hand in hand with prayer but are not prayer, just as cancellation marks on a stamp sometimes distort the stamp's true image. Still other religious practices contain prayer within them. They are similar to bits of envelope that have a stamp on them. Sometimes the extra paper makes the stamp appear to have a different size or shape.

Christians need to understand prayer not as a matter of curiosity, as we might consider a stamp collection. We need to be able to distinguish prayer from other religious practices so we can use it properly. In this respect prayers are more like coins than they are stamps. Our ability to identify what prayer is and what it is not has great practical value.

Imitation Prayers

As a Christian reads his or her Bible, one runs across certain practices that look very much like prayer. We ask ourselves, "Is this prayer, or something else?" It is important for us to identify what appears to be prayer because if we do not do so, our understanding of prayer will be inaccurate and we may not pray as we should.

Wishing

One practice that looks remarkably like prayer and that many people confuse with prayer is wishing. I can remember saying, "I wish I had a million dollars." Is that a prayer? Was the apostle Paul praying when he wrote, "Now may our God and Father himself and Jesus our Lord direct our way to you" (1 Thess. 3:11 RSV)? When Job said, "O that I knew where I might find him!" (23:3 KJV) was that prayer? Those statements are not prayers. The difference between praying and wishing is that in praying we address our communication specifically to God, whereas in wishing we simply voice our desire. I do not mean that wishing is wrong and praying is right. They both have their place, but they are distinct practices.

We often find it hard to distinguish wishes from prayers in the Bible because the person wishing may have God in view even though God is not being addressed. Also, a person may tell God in prayer what he wishes or may request that God grant a wish (a desire or a craving). Moreover, a person may share a desire with another person that he has previously expressed to God in prayer.

The key to the difference between prayers and wishes— and sometimes they are very pious wishes—is the person addressed. Communication to God constitutes prayer, but reflective statements made generally or wishes expressed to another person, or even to no one in particular, are not prayers. That is, the Bible never identifies them as prayers.

Perhaps the most obvious identifying characteristic in a wish in the Bible is the presence of "may," the optative verb tense. This verb usually needs to be supplied, since it is often assumed in a wish (e.g., Rom. 15:5–6; 1 Pet. 5:14). Many of the salutations in the New Testament Epistles are pious wishes (e.g., 1 Cor. 1:2; 2 Tim. 1:2), as are many of the invocations and benedictions. Probably the writer prayed at another time that God's grace and peace would rest upon his readers, but the salutation itself that he wrote is not a prayer. It is the expression of a wish since it does not call on God to grant these graces. This may seem like a fine point, and in a sense it is, but this distinction helps us to understand what prayer is and what it is not. The phrase *blessed is* describes God or someone else. The phrase *blessed be* is part of a wish (Gen. 9:26; Matt. 5:3–11).

In the Old Testament the name of God is often present in the wish: "God forbid . . ." (1 Sam. 24:6), "God judge . . ." (1 Sam. 24:12), "God add . . ." (2 Sam. 24:3 KJV). In the Pauline Epistles grace and peace are the most common subjects of prayerful wishes (e.g., Eph. 1:2). It is amazing that even though pious wishes are not prayers God often responded to them as though they were prayers (e.g., Job 19:23–24). God searches hearts and knows the desires from which wishes spring. Sometimes he graciously grants the desire of the heart even though the person desiring did not express the desire as a prayer to him. Nevertheless he wants us to pray, and we do not have some things because we do not request them in prayer (James 4:2).

Glorying

Another practice that sometimes passes for prayer but is not is what I shall call glorying. Glorying is the practice of uttering doxologies, expressions of praise and thanksgiving about God. Again the crucial difference between these statements and prayers is the person to whom we address them. In a doxology the person speaking talks about God in the third person (him or he) rather than addressing him in the second person (you, thou, or thee).

Doxologies in the Bible usually contain a reason the speaker is blessing God either in the statement itself or in the context of the statement (e.g., Exod. 18:10; Ps. 41:13). Some prayerful wishes closely resemble doxologies because they express the desire that God receive glory (2 Pet. 3:18; Rev. 5:13). Wishes hope that something will happen or will be true, while doxologies state that something has already happened or is already true.

God is the subject of biblical doxologies. The word means the "word of praise," but biblical writers used it of praise spoken of God particularly. The person of God or the work of God is the focus of a doxology. In the Old Testament the acts of God are more frequently the subject of praise in doxologies, whereas in the New Testament the emphasis shifts to his character. Public doxologies are more common in Scripture than private ones. Perhaps by their very nature, doxologies lend themselves to public rather than to private use. Prayer, on the other hand, is equally appropriate in public or in private.

Woes

A third practice of biblical religion that many people confuse with prayer is pronouncing woes. The word *woe* is an interjection that means "alas." Woes may be lamentations of one's own condition (Jer. 15:10) or the condition of another or others (Isa. 3:11). They may also be declarations of coming and assured judgment (Matt. 11:21; Rev. 18:10). The feature that distinguishes them from prayers is that they never appeal to God to act in judgment. Woes are verdicts that announce judgment rather than prayers calling for it (Matt. 23:13). This is true in both the Old and the New Testaments.

Swearing

Swearing sometimes appears to be prayer, but it is not. Swearing, as the Bible refers to it, means affirming that one will indeed do a certain thing or that a certain thing is definitely true. The person making the statement also appeals to God or to some other venerated person or object to add force to the affirmation. The statement itself is an oath. People swear to affirm strongly something that they say.

An oath is not necessarily a prayer. We can make an oath to another person as well as to God. The accompanying appeal is usually a wish rather than a prayer. If the person speaking addresses God, then the oath and the swearing are prayers; but if the person speaking does not address God, they are not.

One common oath form in the Old Testament is, "[May] God do so to me and more also if . . ." This is a pious wish. The declaration of what the speaker swears to do follows negatively: "if I fail to . . ." (1 Sam 20:13; 2 Kings 6:31). Often the appeal is a wish that God will do something to the person swearing if he does not do what he says he will do.

If they are sincere, oaths and their appeals may demonstrate faith in and loyalty to God. The speaker calls on God to witness or to vindicate an action that he or she promises to perform (Rom. 1:9). Nevertheless Jesus Christ taught his disciples to refrain from swearing in everyday speech (Matt. 5:34; cf. James 5:12). The reason is that the Christian's word should not need reinforcing with oaths. It should always be consistently trustworthy and truthful. The Christian's ordinary speech should be as truthful as what he or she speaks under oath. If a person who swears using God's name then breaks the oath, that one uses God's name in vain. He dishonors God as well as himself.

Taking an oath in a court of law is a bit different. There the character of the witness is unknown to the court. To impress the importance of telling the truth on the witness, the court requires the witness to affirm with an oath that he or she will speak only what is true. I do not believe that taking an oath in court violates the spirit of Jesus' command. Jesus appears to have had ordinary everyday speech in mind.

Prayer's Frequent Companions

Certain practices often accompany prayer, as the Scriptures reveal. It is helpful to identify these things because to do so enables us to distinguish prayer from other legitimate practices associated with communication with God. When we recognize the important place that God has given prayer in his plan, we will want to give it its proper place in our lives too. Noticing what often accompanied it in the history of God's people that the Bible records will help us appreciate and promote it today.

Sacrificing

Making sacrifices to God and praying to him have gone hand in hand since people first walked this planet (Gen. 8:20; 12:7–8; 13:4, 18). In the nation of Israel both practices became part of the individual and corporate life of God's people. It is remarkable that the Mosaic law contained no specific instruction about prayer. Evidently prayer was so common, if not frequent, that nothing needed to be said. God took the practice of prayer for granted as a necessary adjunct to sacrificing, probably because prayer accompanied offerings to him even before the Mosaic law.

Prayers accompanied many of the offerings in Israel: the burnt (1 Kings 18:36–37), the evening (Ps. 141:2), the peace (2 Chron. 30:21–22), the firstfruits (Deut. 26:5–10), and the thank offerings (Ps. 56:12–13). Prayers of confession attended the sin and trespass offerings too. The person who brought these offerings had to confess his guilt to God as part of the ritual. God often responded to the prayers offered with sacrifices (2 Chron. 7:1; Dan. 9:20–21). In the future the Jews will evidently reinstitute the five major offerings of the Mosaic system (Ezek. 40:39; 46:3). However, their purpose then seems to be memorial or worshipful rather than atoning. Prayer will doubtless accompany these offerings in the future as it accompanied offerings in the past.

The New Testament writers connected prayer with several Christian offerings including thanksgiving (Eph. 5:20) and praise (Heb. 13:15). Normally we express our personal dedication to God, the offering of ourselves to him, in prayer also (Rom. 6:13; 12:1–2).

This brief review reminds us that prayer has always had close associations with the offerings and sacrifices that constitute such an important part of biblical worship. It is natural when we make a sacrifice to God to express our thoughts and feelings about our offering to God in prayer. The sacrifice is a concrete representation of the desire that we articulate in prayer.

Prayer has a special connection with the sacrifice of Jesus Christ on the cross. We may approach God in prayer because Jesus Christ opened the way for us through his sacrifice for us (1 Tim. 2:5; Heb. 4:16).

Burning Incense

A second practice that goes hand in hand with prayer in the Bible is the burning of incense. Many religions connect the burning of incense with prayer because the sweet-smelling smoke that ascends is similar to prayers arising to God (2 Kings 15:35; cf. Rev. 8:3–4). The Mosaic law specified four spices that the priests were to mix and burn on a special altar (Exod. 30). Only the priests could burn this incense (Num. 16:17; 2 Chron. 26:18). Burning incense was part of the ritual necessary to worship God (1 Chron. 6:49). It accompanied the burnt and peace offerings of worship and the daily morning and evening offerings of dedication, as well as other special offerings presented during the year (1 Kings. 9:25). When Israelites expressed gratitude to God for answering their prayers, the priest burned incense that accompanied their thank offering (Ps. 66:13–14). The prophet Malachi predicted that in the future Gentiles would worship God and burn incense to him in every place (Mal. 1:11). This may be a figurative way of saying that they would pray to him as believers.

There are many interesting parallels between incense and prayer. The Old Testament prescribed the exact composition of incense that was acceptable to God, and in a similar respect the contents of our prayers are important to God. Only the priests in Israel could burn the incense, and now all believer-priests can offer prayer to God. Incense cost the offerer something, and prayer involves some sacrifice and energy. As incense often accompanied other offerings that the Israelites made, so prayer often accompanies other sacrifices that we make. Israel's priests offered incense every morning and evening, and these are still the most popular times for praying. The smoke from the burning incense ascended to heaven, and the prayers of God's people likewise rise from earth to heaven. The incense smelled sweet, and our prayers are pleasing to God. Clearly God intended the burning of incense to be a visual and olfactory aid to teach his people about prayer.

Pouring Water

Pouring water on the ground is another practice that connects with prayer in the Old Testament. This practice occasionally accompanied prayers of confession (1 Sam. 7:5–6; 2 Sam. 14:14; Ps. 22:15; Lam. 2:12). It symbolized deep humiliation. The person who poured water out while praying was expressing his feeling of being unable to get himself together spiritually and perhaps emotionally. The act enabled the worshiper to demonstrate his feelings as well as articulate them.

Casting Lots

Prayer accompanied the casting of lots (sortilege) in Israel's worship for a different reason. In prayer the leaders asked for God's guidance, and by casting lots they received his answer. After the institution of the Aaronic priesthood, the high priest cast lots by using the Urim and Thummim. These were evidently two stones or other small objects that the high priest carried in the breastpiece of his ephod, his ceremonial robe. After praying for God's will, he would reach into the pocket of his garment and draw out one of the objects (1 Sam. 14:41–42). The one he drew out would indicate God's will in a binary fashion. This was not just superstition; God had promised to direct his people in this manner (Prov. 16:33). Sometimes God commanded the Israelites to practice sortilege (Lev. 16:7–10; Num. 26:55–56; Josh. 14:2). At other times the people took the initiative to discover God's will (Josh. 7:14; Judg. 20:9).

It is interesting that the early Christians did not cast lots to determine God's will after the Holy Spirit descended at Pentecost (Acts 2), although they did so shortly before then (Acts 1:24–26). The baptizing work of the Holy Spirit, which joins Christians to the mystical body of Christ, began at Pentecost (1 Cor. 12:13; cf. Acts 11:15). This work continues, then, whenever a person trusts in Jesus Christ for salvation (Rom. 8:9). Jesus promised his disciples that when the Holy Spirit came to indwell them he would provide guidance for them (John 14:26; 16:13). The Holy Spirit first permanently indwelt all believers at Pentecost. Thus the indwelling Holy Spirit replaced the Urim and Thummim after Pentecost.

How we can receive guidance in decision making from the Holy Spirit troubles any sincere Christian who wants to do God's will. Since the Holy Spirit guided holy men to write the Scriptures (2 Pet. 1:21; 2 Tim. 3:16), the Bible is the primary source of guidance for Christians. However, the Holy Spirit also indwells every true Christian (Rom. 8:9). In the areas of decision making that the Scriptures do not address, the Spirit can provide subjective direction. He can guide any believer who sincerely wants to walk in God's ways. Many of the mundane decisions that we make do not require special direction from God. We can make those choices in dependence on him and trust that he is leading us if we are not violating the revealed will of God. Many of our choices are amoral; they do not involve choosing between something that is in harmony with or contrary to God's moral will.

Obtaining God's guidance through either modern or ancient means should always include prayer. In prayer for guidance we humble ourselves before God and express our need for his direction. We ask for his will and for his enablement to do his will. To seek for God's direction without praying for it is like trying to find out what the boss wants us to do without asking him.

Laying On Hands

In both the Old and New Testaments, prayer frequently accompanied the practice of laying hands on people. This custom visually and tangibly symbolized identification with a person, transference of something intangible to him or her, and devotion to God.

In Old Testament times, people laid hand on others when performing acts of blessing (Gen. 48:14), sacrificing (Exod. 29:10), and bearing witness in cases of capital offense (Lev. 24:14). The imposition of hands marked the Levites as a special group (Num. 8:10). Moses also consecrated Joshua as his successor with this practice (Num. 27:18; Deut. 34:9).

Jesus blessed the children (Matt. 19:13, 15) and healed the sick (Matt. 9:18; Mark 6:5) by laying his hands on them. The apostles laid hand on others when they imparted the Holy Spirit (Acts 8:17, 19; 19:6) and when they healed them (Acts 28:8). The early Christians employed this custom when they set individuals aside to special ministries (Acts 6:6; 13:3; 1 Tim. 4:14; 2 Tim. 1:6). Authorized representatives likewise recognized spiritual leaders as such in the churches by laying hands on them (1 Tim. 4:14; 5:22; Heb. 6:2).

This rite involved no magic. It symbolized the transference of a Person (i.e., the Holy Spirit, Acts 6:6; 8:15–17) or a power (2 Tim. 1:6) from God to an individual. It illustrated a divine blessing that prayer, which accompanied the rite, articulated. Prayer sought, obtained, and expressed gratitude for the favor. The laying on of hands made visual its bestowal.

Dedicating

Dedicating in the biblical sense involves the act of setting anything or anyone aside to the worship or service of God. Prayer is the instrument one uses to present this resolution to God. Prayer accompanied the dedication of Solomon's temple (1 Kings 8:22–55, 62–64) and Nehemiah's wall (Neh. 12:40–42). After returning from exile in Babylon, the Jews dedicated themselves anew to God and expressed this resolve in prayer (2 Chron. 29:28–30). Christians should dedicate themselves to God in view of what he has done for us (Rom. 6:13; 12:1–2). We normally express this dedication to God in prayer (Rom. 6:16; 2 Cor. 8:5).

Dedication involves a fundamental change of attitude and a resolution to obey God (Isa. 6:8; Acts 22:10). While the words we say to God when we dedicate ourselves or something else to him are obviously important, even more important is our follow-through (Mal. 1:9; James 4:2–10).

Repenting

Repenting has clear connections with dedicating, and prayer normally accompanies it too. It is difficult to understand the biblical concept of repenting because the word has taken on connotations through English usage that it does not have in the original Greek of the New Testament. In English, repentance connotes a change of behavior. We are accustomed to preachers calling for repentance, and we understand them to mean that they want us to clean up our lives. While this is a legitimate concern that comes out of the Bible, it skews our understanding of the biblical call to repentance.

The Greek word translated "repent" (*metanoeo*) comes from two words that mean "to think again." Repentance focuses primarily on the mental change that should result in a change of behavior. When John the Baptist was calling on people to repent because the kingdom of heaven was at hand, he was urging them to change their way of thinking (Matt. 3:2). They had been thinking that the kingdom was far away temporally. They needed to realize that it was very close because the King had already arrived and was about to begin his ministry. Multitudes went out to John to hear him preach in the wilderness and to allow him to baptize them as a sign of their acceptance of and their identification with his message. Pharisees also came to John. They were claiming to have repented, but they had not. Therefore John called on them to bring forth fruits worthy of repentance. He challenged them to demonstrate in their behavior that they had really changed their minds. This distinction between repentance (the change of mind) and the fruits of repentance (the change of behavior) is an important one to observe. Repentance is a change of mind—about sin, God, oneself, or something else. Keeping this biblical use of the word in mind helps us to understand what the biblical writers meant went they wrote about it and what the speakers who used the word meant.

Prayer accompanies repenting in the same sense as it accompanies dedicating. It expresses a personal internal transaction. Repentance is the attitude that expresses itself in confessing guilt (Num. 5:7), requesting forgiveness (Exod. 34:9; 2 Sam. 24:10), and casting oneself on God's mercy (Judg. 3:9; Joel 2:12–14).

We should never confuse or equate a prayer of confession with repentance. It is only the articulation of repentance. Prayer is no substitute for repentance either. The attitude of the heart must be present first or the words from the lips will be hollow and meaningless. The condition of our heart is more important than the words in our mouth.

Fasting

People fast for a variety of reasons. Some do it for purely physical reasons, for example, to purge their bodies of impurities. Others do it for mental purposes, to clear their thoughts so they can concentrate better. Still others fast for a variety of psychological reasons. In the Bible, however, fasting always has spiritual connections. It has to do with a person's relationship with God. Fasting usually occurred with prayer, although most commonly people prayed without fasting. The purpose of fasting for spiritual reasons was to devote the time and energy normally spent eating and drinking to a higher purpose. It was a way of obtaining more time for prayer when the people involved believed that talking to God was a more pressing need than fueling their bodies.

Scripture is clear that fasting in itself will not move God to do things that he would not do otherwise. Fasting is, in a sense, one of the fruits of repentance. It expresses physically what is inside a person's heart and mind. When I was in college I read a book that gave me the impression that if I would fast God would answer more of my prayers. I thought I had discovered a great secret to spiritual power. I set aside the following weekend and determined to fast until God saved a particular individual that I had a burden for. That person did not become a Christian that weekend, but I learned an important lesson. People cannot manipulate God by fasting. God has not promised that he will give us whatever we want when we fast.

Fasting does demonstrate how strongly we feel about what we are praying about. It enables us to concentrate in prayer and to call on God with unusual intensity to answer. This intense asking based on intense desire is what moves God. He remains sovereign and will not abdicate his authority by caving in to the petitions of fasters, but those prayers do affect him. Asking will get us things that failing to ask will not (James 4:2). Asking persistently will get us things that casual asking will not because persistent asking manifests faith (Luke 18:1–8).

If your child asks you for something, you will consider giving it to him or her because you love your child and want to bless him or her. However, your decision to give, to delay giving, or to withhold what the child requests depends on many factors, only some of which your child appreciates. If your child persistently asks you for the same thing, you realize that this matter is important to him or her. This realization will incline you further to grant the request, but only if it is in the best interest of your child. Similarly, fasting can demonstrate to God how much we want what we ask. It will not force him to grant our petition, but it will incline him to do so more than if we did not fast.

Occasional fasting is natural when a Christian prays faithfully and earnestly. God does not command us to fast, but if you feel a need very greatly you may want to skip a meal to pray about it. Skipping a meal will give you additional time to pray, and it will show God how much you want what you are requesting.

In Old Testament times fasting also expressed sorrow. People who felt very sorry because of their sins sometimes went without food temporarily to demonstrate that sorrow to God in prayer (2 Sam. 3:35; Judg. 20:26–28; Esther 4:3). As we might expect, fasting often accompanied prayers of confession (2 Chron. 20:3–13) and repentance (Jon. 3:5–10). The fact that fasting frequently took place in sackcloth and with ashes on the head (Dan. 9:3–19; Joel 1:13–14) illustrates the penitential attitude of those who fasted. Sometimes prostration on the ground also accompanied it (2 Sam. 12:16).

God commanded the Israelites to fast once a year on the Day of Atonement (Lev. 16:31). As time passed, other fasts became traditional in Israel. The contrition associated with these fasts unfortunately became formal and hypocritical (Isa. 58:1–9; Matt. 9:14–17). Thus a wholesome practice deteriorated. Jesus never discouraged voluntary fasting, but he had no use for hypocritically going without food to make a pious impression on other people (Matt. 6:16–18).

The textual problem in Mark 9:29 has troubled some students of prayer. The context describes Jesus coming down the mountain on which he had been transfigured to find his disciples unable to cast a demon out of a boy. The disciples had previously cast demons out of many people, but this case proved too difficult for them. When they asked Jesus why they had been unsuccessful, he responded that this kind of case required prayer. Some ancient manuscripts have "prayer and fasting." It is very difficult to determine if "and fasting" was in the original autograph of Mark's Gospel. I tend to think it was not, because of the manuscript evidence. Probably a scribe added it because situations involving much prayer often elicited fasting in Judaism and in the early church. In any case Jesus' point is clear. Some cases of satanic opposition are so strong that they require more prayer than others do for victory. The addition of "and fasting" in some manuscripts confirms the point that fasting indicated intense praying in the early church.

The note of earnestness present in the biblical record of Old Testament fasting persists in the New Testament instances of it, but the element of sorrow seems less prominent (Acts 13:2–6; 14:23). Fasting was a normal attendant to fervent persistent prayer in the early church. Voluntary, unostentatious fasting for a spiritual purpose has always been acceptable to God, and it still is today.

The length of a fast is of secondary importance. Scripture records fasts of various lengths: forty days and nights (Exod. 34:28; Matt. 4:2), three weeks (Dan. 10:2–3), seven days (1 Sam. 31:13), three days (Esther 4:16; Acts 9:9), and shorter periods. The important thing is not how long one goes without physical nourishment. It is that the time spent fasting, regardless of length, be a voluntary setting aside of physical needs to give oneself to spiritual renewal through prayer. Sometimes the Word of God and prayer are more necessary than food (Matt. 4:4). Persistent fervent prayer may result in fasting, but fasting without prayer has little spiritual value. Obviously it could have some other value. Fasting for spiritual reasons should always be a means to a higher end and never an end in itself.

Watching

Watching is a practice associated with prayer in the Bible that is very similar to fasting. Fasting involves going without food to concentrate on praying. Watching describes keeping awake or alert. Watching means going without sleep to concentrate on prayer.

The New Testament describes watchfulness in three different relationships to prayer. First, Jesus Christ commanded Peter, James, and John to watch and pray (Matt. 26:38–39). He explained that by doing so they could avoid entering into the temptation that they would experience if they failed to pray (Matt. 26:40–42). In this sense watching involves a battle. I have found that I can concentrate in prayer more easily if I pray aloud and if I vary my habits of praying occasionally.

Second, Christians should watch (be on the alert) that we do not carelessly neglect prayer but faithfully persist in it (Eph. 6:18). This is slightly different from the former responsibility. It is not so much failing to continue praying as it is failing to pray at all because we see no need for it. Jesus reminded his disciples that persistence in prayer often results in answers to prayer that would not be forthcoming otherwise (Luke 21:36). Paul stayed up late at night praying because he believed that praying would bring God's blessing on the people for whom he prayed (2 Cor. 6:5; cf. James 4:2).

Third, we read that we should add watchfulness to our prayers, as an essential ingredient in a recipe. Along with praying we need to remain watchful to what is going on around us. We need to keep alert to other matters (Col. 4:2–4). Jesus told his disciples to keep their eyes open to see how the times were corresponding with his predictions, and to keep on praying (Mark 13:33–37). Another ingredient that should be present is thanksgiving (Col. 4:2–4). To summarize the scriptural injunctions concerning watchfulness, we should pray, and keep alert when we pray, and keep alert because we pray. Obviously it is important that we combine watchfulness with prayer.

Reading Scripture

Prayer and the Word of God go hand in hand in the Christian life, as well as in Scripture. This is only reasonable since in prayer we speak to God and in the Bible he speaks to us. Prayer and the Scriptures are the vehicles by which we enjoy communication with God. Prayer is the term that the Bible uses to describe our side of the conversation, and Scripture contains God's most important words to us.

In the very early history of humanity God spoke directly to people. As time progressed, he spoke to people and preserved the record of his dealings with mankind in Scripture. Eventually he stopped giving special revelation because he had revealed all that he wanted to say. Christians have long believed that the Bible contains everything that is spiritually essential for life and godliness (2 Tim. 3:16–17). All the crucial spiritual answers that people want and that God wants us to have stand recorded in the Bible. We need to study its pages to find the answers to life's great questions.

Bible reading often leads to conviction of sin that should result in confession in prayer (Neh. 9:1–4; 1 Cor. 11:28). Conversely, prayer is excellent preparation for reading God's Word (Neh. 8:6). We also need to pray for divine enablement when we discover God's will in his Word (Acts 4:24–31). Both prayer and Bible reading are necessary practices for the reception of God's good gifts (1 Tim. 4:4–5), and both are indispensable for spiritual growth (Jude 20; Acts 20:32; 2 Tim. 3:17).

Singing

Prayer and the singing of songs to God accompany one another too. Since psalms, hymns, and spiritual songs are frequently expressions of praise, they often contain prayers (Col. 3:16). Psalms refer to the inspired poems in the Bible that God's people used in their private and public worship. Hymns are modern songs that express similar sentiments, although they are not on the level of inspired Scripture. Spiritual songs are songs that deal with spiritual subjects. They tend to focus on personal experience and testimony; hymns normally deal with the person and work of God.

The Psalter contains many different types of psalms: praise, lament, prophetic, didactic, penitential, imprecatory, and others. In some praise and thanksgiving predominate, while others exhort the reader to praise and thank God. Some contain petitions for self and others. Usually a psalm contains several different characteristics including many varieties of prayer, but sometimes one sentiment pervades the entire composition. Many psalms are prayers partially or wholly. "That which really, in the last analysis occurs in the Psalms is prayer" (Claus Westermann, *The Praise of God in the Psalms*, translated by Keith R. Crum [Richmond: John Knox, 1965], 24).

One psalm that is obviously a prayer, Hannah's psalm, appears in 1 Samuel 2:1–10. This psalm contains no petitions, yet the writer of 1 Samuel labeled it a prayer. Another prayer in a psalm occurs in Psalm 6, which is typical of many psalms in this respect. The main part of that psalm is prayer (vv. 1–7). Jonah 2:1–9 contains testimony, praise, and thanksgiving, but the writer called it a prayer. The writer of Habakkuk 3:1–19 called it a prayer, and it is also a psalm. Songs of praise were also prayers (Ps. 42:8). The inspired ancient editors of the Psalter grouped and called the first two books of psalms (Pss. 1–72), "the prayers of David" (Ps. 72:20). This title refers to most if not all the psalms that precede it. The Jews used the Hallel (lit. praise) psalms (Pss. 113–18; 136) as part of their prayers at Passover (cf. Matt. 26:30). These psalms contain prayers that the Jews and early Christians sang as hymns.

Paul and Silas prayed and sang praises to God in the Philippian jail (Acts 16:25). The Greek verb and participle used to describe their action indicate that their singing was praying. They were praying to God in song. Many modern hymns also voice prayers or contain prayers. For example, "Break Thou the Bread of Life" and "Fairest Lord Jesus" are prayers set to music.

Singing hymns and spiritual songs is a natural and joyful way to praise and thank God. The Spirit-filled Christian typically sings to God within himself or herself giving thanks for all things (Eph. 5:20; Col. 3:16). Christians who feel in good spirits should sing praises to God (James 5:13). Believers who are in distress should cast their burden on the Lord in prayer (Ps. 57:1; 1 Pet. 5:7). Both praise and petition can be sung as well as simply spoken. The music can often help express the mood.

Practices That Include Prayer

Three other practices of the Christian faith have close connection with prayer. These practices do not merely accompany prayer; rather, prayer constitutes an integral part of these practices.

Worshiping

Webster's *New World Dictionary* defines worship as "extreme devotion; intense love or admiration of any kind." In this sense, we could say that one individual might worship another. Proper worship, however, always has God as its object. Thus the *International Standard Bible Encyclopedia* defines worship in the Bible as "honor, reverence, homage, in thought, feeling, or act, made to men, angels, or other 'spiritual' beings, and figuratively to other entities, ideas, powers or qualities, but specifically and expressly to

Deity." Worship involves giving God the honor that he is
worthy of receiving because of who he is and what he has
done (Acts 27:23–24; Phil. 3:3).

There are many ways in which we can worship God.
These include voicing public testimony to God's goodness
(Deut. 25:5–10; 1 Kings 3:6–9) and announcing publicly
what he will do before he does it (1 Kings 18:36–37). It
involves praising God with musical instruments (2 Chron.
29:28), knowing God and following him faithfully (Hos.
6:6), fasting (Luke 2:37), and presenting ourselves to him
as living sacrifices (Rom. 12:1–2). Perhaps the most simple and common way of worshiping God is by praying to
him.

Scripture records that God's people offered worship and
prayer to the Lord individually (Job 1:21; Dan. 2:46) and
corporately (Ezra 3:11; Neh. 9:1–4). They did so in the early
church as well as in Israel (Col. 4:2–4; 1 Tim. 2:1–4). Many
corporate acts of worship that included prayer included
praise to God specifically (Exod. 15:1–19; 2 Sam. 15:32).

The German commentator Franz Delitzsch called prayer
"the soul of all worship" (*Biblical Commentary on the
Prophecies of Isaiah*, [Edinburgh: T & T Clark, 1890],
2:363). One of the Greek words for prayer that appears most
frequently on the pages of the New Testament, *proseu-
chomai*, often means worship. Prayer in some form is foundational to all true worship of God.

The true God is the supreme object of worship in biblical revelation. In the Old Testament, people worshiped God
with very little distinction between the persons of the Godhead. This was because God had not revealed much about
the nature of his triune being then. In the New Testament,
however, as revelation increased (particularly with the
teachings of Jesus), we read of people worshiping the individual members of the Trinity.

Jesus taught his disciples to address God the Father in prayer (Matt. 6:9). In the early church, Christians frequently addressed their prayers to the risen Christ, calling him "Lord" (Acts 2:21, 36; 4:24, 29; 8:22; 1 Cor. 1:2). A few verses seem to support the idea that we may pray to the Holy Spirit, but most commentators have rejected the interpretations that lead to this conclusion (Eph. 6:18; Phil. 3:3; Jude 20). Nevertheless, it seems proper to pray to the Holy Spirit for two reasons: first, since the Holy Spirit is God, praying to the Holy Spirit amounts to praying to God; second, each member of the divine Trinity stands in immediate relationship to the individual believer, since each is supreme in his own work. Each member of the Godhead is properly an object of worship and therefore a legitimate object for Christians' prayers. The scriptural emphasis and natural practice are nevertheless that prayer should normally be to the Father in the name of the Son and in the power of the Holy Spirit (John 16:23; Jude 20). This is so because of the administrative order within the Godhead. The Spirit glorifies the Son, and the Son glorifies the Father.

What caused people to worship God by praying to him? Usually some revelation that God made or some work that he performed generated worship and prayer. A new revelation of God that he gave his people frequently elicited their worship (Exod. 12:27; 33:10; 34:8; Lev. 9:24; Josh. 5:13–15; 2 Chron. 7:1–3; 20:3–13). Other causes of worship are answered prayer (Gen. 24:26–27; 1 Sam. 1:19–20; 1 Kings 18:36–37), God's faithfulness to his promises (Deut. 26:5–10), and his assurances of enablement (Judg. 6:22; 7:15). Spiritual revival also produced renewed worship and revitalized prayer (2 Chron. 29:28–30).

The Scriptures frequently record that a person worshiped God on the top of a mountain or a hill, or at some other elevated site (2 Sam. 15:32; 24:21). The idea behind praying there seems to have been to get as close to heaven and God as possible. Jesus Christ taught that the physical place of worship is not as important as one's mental and heart attitude in prayer and worship (John 4:20–24).

Often the biblical writers described worship in terms of the posture that the worshiper assumed in prayer (Heb. 11:21). The most common posture was bowing oneself down toward the ground (Exod. 20:4–5; 2 Kings 17:35–36; 2 Chron. 25:14; Zech. 14:16–17). Sometimes the person praying bowed his or her whole body over (Ps. 95:6; Mic. 6:6; Heb. 13:18). Not infrequently worshipers prostrated themselves in prayer before the Lord (Lev. 9:24; Dan. 2:46; 1 Cor. 14:25; Rev. 4:10–11). Most often the person worshiping just bowed his or her head in worship (Exod. 2:23–25; 1 Chron. 29:20; Neh. 8:6; 9:1–4). Sometimes people raised their hands in prayer to illustrate their honor for God or their desire to receive a blessing from him.

Posture in prayer by itself has no power with God. It reflects the attitudes that the person praying holds toward God and himself or herself. The most common postures are similar to how one would approach a sovereign in biblical times. The greater the worshiper's concept of his sovereign's person and might, and the more clearly he perceived his own subject and helpless condition by comparison, the humbler was that one's physical approach.

The most important principle involving posture in prayer seems to be this: Posture does not determine the effectiveness of our prayers, but it does reflect how we view God, ourselves, and our relationship with God. Thus our posture may indicate an appropriate or inappropriate approach to God in worship and prayer.

Since prayer occupies such a prominent place in worship, what is true of our worship will often be true of our prayers. The purpose, objects, causes, and characteristics of our worship will usually be those of our prayers. This is especially true of prayers of praise and thanksgiving since these are the kinds that we use most in our worship.

Vowing

Another religious practice that includes prayer is making a vow to God. Webster's dictionary defines a vow as "a solemn promise or pledge; especially one to God, or a god, dedicating oneself to an act, service, or way of life." A more biblical definition would be this: A vow is a formal promise to set aside and give oneself or something to the Lord to get something from him or because he has already given something. When a person makes a vow, he or she expresses a resolution to God in prayer after the person has determined to do what he or she promises.

The Bible describes two types of vows: conditional and unconditional. In an unconditional vow, the person vowing places no condition on God to do or not do something before the person will fulfill the vow. Vows of this kind consist of simple pledges to do something, such as separating from sin or offering a sacrifice to the Lord. The Nazarite vow illustrates this unconditional type of vow (Num. 6:1–21). By taking a Nazarite vow, an Israelite could commit himself to living as a priest for a certain time that he normally determined. Samson was an exception. The Lord determined that he should be a Nazarite all his life (Judg. 13:5). Nazarite vows were voluntary in Israel, but once a person had taken this vow God expected him to fulfill it (cf. Lev. 27; Eccles. 5:4–5).

In a conditional vow, the person vowing made a request as well as a promise. He promised that if God would do a specified thing then he would do something else in return (Num. 21:2; 1 Sam. 1:10–11; 2 Sam. 15:8; Ps. 66:13). Vowing in this manner constitutes bargaining with God (Gen. 28:20–22; Judg. 11:30). Often the promise made is that if

God will grant the request the person vowing will praise and thank him (Ps. 7:17; 56:12–13; Nah. 1:15). Occasionally the person vowing pledges something more tangible and costly (Judg. 11:30–31). Usually individuals made vows in Scripture, but in a few cases a group made a corporate pledge to God (Judg. 10:10; 1 Sam. 12:10).

Vowing was always voluntary in the Bible; God never commanded people to take vows nor did he prohibit them from doing so (Deut. 23:21–23; Judg. 11:30). He wants promises that people make to him to arise out of their own hearts. Even though they are voluntary, God regards the making of a vow, which is a strong promise, as a serious commitment (Ps. 76:11; Eccles. 5:4–6; Nah. 1:15).

Instances of vowing that the Bible records usually resulted from great earnestness and fervency in prayer. If one's heart overflowed with love and appreciation to God, he or she made an unconditional vow (Ps. 57:9–10; 59:16–17). Conversely, when a person strongly desired something from the Lord, he or she would make a promise to do something for God if he would grant the request (Gen. 28:20–22; Jon. 1:14; 2:1–9).

There are more biblical vows in the Old Testament than in the New Testament. Yet some of the early Christians did make vows to God. The apostle Paul bound himself with a vow at least twice (Acts 18:18), as did four other unnamed Christians (Acts 21:23).

There is nothing wrong with vowing. Jesus' negative references to vows were condemnations of their abuse, not their use (Matt. 15:4–5; Mark 7:10–13). However, the scarcity of vows, especially conditional vows, in the New Testament should warn us against making them often. The Old Testament particularly reveals that people who made vows to God sometimes made foolish promises that they wished they had not made, or they failed to keep their promises to God. This insight into human foolishness and unfaithfulness should make us pause before vowing something to God. We have a natural tendency to break our promises and should therefore cast ourselves and our requests on God's grace rather than bargaining with him (Matt. 26:39).

Christian leaders should be cautious about calling on God's people, especially immature young people, to make pledges to God for foreign missionary service or full-time ministry, for example. Sincere young people may make promises to God, for instance, at an emotional campfire service. Then they may face confusion later in life when they believe God is leading them to do something different from what they promised. This can result in terrible internal tension and may even lead an adult to abandon a mature evaluation of God's leading in favor of an immature vow.

Vowing, even though it may be imprudent, is popular and will probably continue forever (Isa. 19:20–21).

Requesting Signs

When the Bible refers to a sign from God it is referring to an object or an incident that people regard as a demonstration of divine power. It involves a special situation by which God reveals himself or his will. In the past, God sometimes gave a sign spontaneously without anyone asking him to give it (Gen. 9:9–16; Isa. 7:12–25). More commonly, however, he gave a sign in response to a prayer of petition (Josh. 10:12–14; Matt. 24:29–30).

In some cases, the sign that God gave, whether sought or not, involved a change of circumstances that identified his will to the person praying (Gen. 24:12–15; 1 Sam. 14:9–10). Other signs contravened the laws of nature (Judg. 6:36–40; 2 Kings 20:8–11). People who requested this second type of sign usually sought definite confirmation from

God that he would indeed do a certain thing (2 Chron. 32:24). Biblical personalities saw the sign as a divine pledge that something else would happen.

In biblical times, when God was still giving authoritative new revelation for all people, he did not discourage people from requesting either kind of sign provided they were sincere (Exod. 3:18; 4:1; Judg. 6:37–39; Luke 5:1–11; John 6:26). Once God even commanded King Ahaz to ask him for a sign (Isa. 7:12). Jesus refused to multiply signs for the scribes and Pharisees because they refused to believe the clear evidence of his deity that he had already given them including many signs (Luke 11:29–32).

Today God does not normally violate the laws of nature to give a person a sign confirming what he has said, especially when the Scriptures are available to the person seeking reassurance. There is ample evidence in the Bible that God can and will do what he has said, so the additional confirmation of a miracle is usually unnecessary (Luke 16:31). If a person needs stronger faith, he or she should hear and believe the Word of God (Rom. 10:17). Miraculous signs do not produce strong faith. Immediately after witnessing the ten plagues and the parting of the Red Sea, the Israelites failed to trust God several times (Exod. 15:22–17:7). Likewise Jesus' critics did not believe in him despite the many miracles he did demonstrating that he was God.

Asking God to arrange circumstances in a fashion that we dictate is not a good idea either. It is interesting that there are no prayers of this type in the Book of Acts, the only exception being Acts 1:24–26, which I discussed earlier in this chapter. It is clear, however, that the early Christians sometimes viewed circumstances as indicators by which God made his will known to them (Acts 16:6–7; Rom. 1:13). God sometimes reveals his will, among other ways, by opening and closing doors of opportunity (i.e., through circumstances, Acts 16:7; 1 Cor. 16:9). For example, a missionary candidate who has done everything to get to the field and still cannot do so—because of insufficient support, lack of a visa, or whatever—might conclude that God has shut the door. As we sincerely attempt to discern God's will from the Scriptures, the Holy Spirit gives individual guidance. Sometimes he does this by controlling circumstances. However, circumstances may or may not be signs of God's will (Acts 16:7). We should, therefore, base our decisions on objective scriptural directives and principles more than on our subjective interpretation of circumstances. I believe that God sometimes uses circumstances to clarify his will, but it is always hard to determine whether a circumstance is a divine sign or a coincidence.

Many Christians believe that if they pray about an amoral decision, God will indicate his will by giving them peace about the right decision. They usually base this practice on Philippians 4:6–7. But notice that these verses do not promise that when we decide what is God's will he will identify it as such by giving us peace. What these verses do promise is that God will give us peace when we pray about what tempts us to feel anxious. The peace of God is the consequence of praying about our anxieties. It is not necessarily the indicator of God's will. Some Christians have decided to do something that was contrary to God's will because they prayed about it and felt peace. They were mistaken. God does often confirm his will by giving peace to those who pray about it and then commit to doing it.

Colossians 3:15 is sometimes a problem too. There Paul exhorted his readers to choose what will result in peace between ourselves and others, especially God, when we face choices. He did not say that peace will always indicate the right choice when we face decisions. Making wise decisions requires investigating the Scriptures (Ps. 119:105), praying for God's wisdom (James 1:5), and seeking the objective insight of other godly believers who can help us evaluate our options (Prov. 15:22). It is not just a matter of feeling peace.

As we have seen, there are many practices within Christianity that have a close relationship to prayer. In some of these, prayer plays an indispensable part. Prayer almost inevitably accompanies other practices. Still other practices appear to be prayer but are something different. Sorting these things out gives us a biblical understanding of prayer and helps us to practice it as God intended.

1 Chronicles 4:10

Jabez cried out to the God of Israel, "Oh, that you would bless me and enlarge my territory! Let your hand be with me, and keep me from harm so that I will be free from pain." And God granted his request.

2 Chronicles 20:12

"O our God, will you not judge them? For we have no power to face this vast army that is attacking us. We do not know what to do, but our eyes are upon you."

4

Prayer in the Old Testament

My uncle Richard—we called him Uncle Rich—was a fascinating person. When I was a boy, our family would occasionally drive down from Chicago to visit him in St. Louis. Uncle Rich lived in the Victorian house in which he had been born late in the nineteenth century. The house had outbuildings, a peach orchard, a well from which we drew drinking water, and most fascinating of all, a woodworking shop in the cellar. Uncle Rich was an engraver by trade—one of the last hand engravers before machines greatly reduced the number of people who practiced his art. He was a skilled painter too. Whenever we would visit him, I loved to go down into his workshop and watch him create something on his lathe.

Uncle Rich would put a rough block of walnut or cherry wood on the lathe and fasten it in place. Then he would turn the machine on and I would watch the wood whirl in a formless blur. He would then take a chisel in hand, rest it on the guide, and bring it into contact with the edges of that whirling mass. The chips would fly everywhere. Before he was finished we would both be covered with chips and sawdust. As I watched, he would begin to turn that blur into a cylinder. Then he would take other chisels and cut grooves in the cylinder. Some parts of the cylinder would be bigger around than others as he deliberately cut away at it. He knew exactly what the finished piece would look like because he had an image of it in his mind, but to me it was a mystery unfolding. Was he making a lamp base, or a dish, or a bowl, or something else? I could only wait and see.

Our understanding of prayer is similar to my predicament as I watched Uncle Rich at work creating on his lathe. We see only a part of what the Master Craftsman is producing. As we give it our careful attention, we gain greater understanding of what he intends it to be.

If we would start reading the Bible in Genesis and read it chronologically, in the order in which God revealed each book, we would see God's intention for prayer developing. If we read only Genesis, we might conclude some things about prayer that would be inaccurate. I would have done this if I had not stayed with Uncle Rich until he had put the finishing touch on his trophy and taken it off his lathe. Likewise, if we read only the Gospels we would not understand prayer as God intended it. If I dropped in on my uncle after he had started his project and left soon afterward, I would not appreciate it as I would if I stuck with him from beginning to end. I might conclude from my limited observation that he intended it for one purpose whereas he really meant it for another.

A correct understanding of prayer requires consideration of all that God has revealed about it in his Word. It also requires that we appreciate that God revealed his will concerning prayer progressively through Scripture. The purpose of this chapter is to trace the significant new revelation about prayer that God unveiled as history unfolded so we can understand and appreciate it as we should.

God revealed the doctrine of prayer, like most other biblical teachings, progressively through the course of history.

Prayers recorded in the first books of the Bible differ significantly from those in the later books. Development of the doctrine is evident as one reads through Scripture.

Prayer in Early Human History

For the purposes of our survey, this period begins with the creation of the cosmos and ends with the creation of the nation of Israel. The main sources of our information on this era are the books of Genesis and Job.

The first biblical prayer probably appears in Genesis 3:9–13. Here Adam expressed his thoughts and feelings to God. This may not have been the first time Adam spoke to God, but it is the first such instance that the Bible records. This prayer was Adam's part in an intimate conversation with his creator. Adam was a fallen creature when he uttered this first prayer. It was a prayer of general narration in which Adam reported his actions to God. The fall was its cause. If Adam had not chosen to sin, he would not have prayed this prayer.

This prayer is a bit different from most prayers since Moses described God's conversation with Adam as face to face. Most prayer involves speaking to the invisible God. Moses may have described the conversation this way to dramatize it. But since God often appeared to the patriarchs in visible form, it seems that Adam probably saw a manifestation of God in human form or at least heard an audible voice. This theophany does not make Adam's part of the conversation anything less than prayer, however, since he was addressing God.

Prayer may have accompanied the first sacrifice recorded in the Bible (Gen. 4:4) as it frequently did later sacrifices, although the writer did not state that. If it did, the cause for the prayer would have been the fall and the sinful condition of Adam and Eve that resulted from it.

Genesis 4:26 appears to most readers to be the first reference to prayer in the Bible. However, calling upon the name of the Lord elsewhere in Scripture usually describes worship. Prayer plays such a prominent role in worship throughout the Bible that it is reasonable to assume that prayer was involved in the worship that this verse describes. Moses probably documented the commencement of habitual prayer and worship at this point in human history. It was Seth's branch of the human family that worshiped God. Moses evidently mentioned that here because a life of worship and prayer marked a distinction between the godly and the wicked in the branches of Adam's family that developed.

Why did the descendants of Seth call on the Lord? As the number of humans increased, the influence of the fall and human sin became more obvious. Some humans recognized their need for God and began to seek his presence and his help seriously and consistently. Abel's offering may have been private (Gen. 4:4), but this worship was public. Thus at this very early stage in human history, perhaps the third generation, we see human beings sensing their need for divine enablement as a result of the fall. They called on God repeatedly in worship and prayer.

It is not my intention to point out all the references to prayer in the Bible. What follows is what I believe to be the most significant references to prayer in God's record of human history, significant in that they help us to understand prayer.

The first answer to a prayer of inquiry appears in Genesis 15:4–5. Having received promises that God would bless him and make him a blessing, Abram asked God in prayer to clarify how he would do that. The Lord responded by giving the patriarch another promise (Gen. 15:5) and by making an unconditional covenant with him (Gen. 15:9–21). These revelations came in answer to Abram's inquiries (cf. Gen. 15:2–3, 8). Abram believed God's promise, and God counted him as righteous for believing it. He received the confirming covenant that has been the basis of God's dealings with humankind ever since that day. Thus Abram's prayer had far-reaching effects. God gave Abram much more than he had requested. As Scripture unfolds, we note that this is often the way God responds to the petitions of those who trust him (see, e.g., 1 Sam. 1:11; 2:21). God's answer also constituted a strong encouragement for Abram to ask again in prayer.

Hagar, too, discovered that God hears the cries of the needy when they are in distress (Gen. 16:11). Yahweh responded to her need with a promise of a son. Prayers often express our felt needs to God. It is those needs that God sees and to which he responds (Gen. 16:13). God observes the human condition including our afflictions, and he normally comes to the aid of those who call on him for help. This is the first of many such prayers that the Bible documents (Job 13:23–24; Ps. 4:1; 5:1; 12:1; Rev. 6:9–10).

The first intercessory prayer appears in Genesis 17:18. Abraham requested that Ishmael might live before God and be the channel through whom God would provide his promised blessings to the world. This is also the first record of a petition denied (Gen. 17:19). The reason for the denial was that God wanted to do something better for Abraham than what he had requested. This is another theme that runs through Scripture. God delights to give people more blessings than they know how to request or dare to expect. Abraham's intercession was successful, however, because God blessed Ishmael as a result of it (Gen. 17:20). Intercession usually results in God acting for the welfare of another person, as he did here.

The importance of persistence in prayer appears first in Genesis 18:23–33. Elsewhere in Scripture we see that persistence in prayer is necessary to obtain some blessings. In this account of Abraham interceding for the righteous in Sodom, the reason for persistence in prayer is clear. Abraham persisted because he felt a need very strongly, namely, that God would not dishonor his name by destroying the righteous with the wicked (Gen. 18:23–25). When we do not persist, it is often because we do not believe that our request is urgent. This sense of need is at the root of all prayer—self-sufficient people rarely pray—but it is especially evident in cases of persistent prayer.

We can see the same urgent need in Jacob's persistent prayer in Genesis 32:26–29. Two other important aspects of prayer also surface in this story. The first is that fervency in prayer is also a result of some deeply felt need (Gen. 32:9–12). The second is that effectiveness in prayer has some connection with fervency as well as with persistence. Fervently laying hold of God, as Jacob did, often happens when one realizes how desperately he or she needs God's help. It is difficult to be fervent in prayer when we feel that our request is only mildly important. However, when fear of not obtaining the needed favor grips us, we pray fervently. God answers such requests by giving us what is best (Matt. 7:7–11).

Another new revelation about prayer during this period of history appears in the Book of Job. One of the problems that Job experienced during his testing by Satan was God's silence. He could not get answers to his prayers (Job 7:11–21; 12:4). Finally God broke his silence and explained that this patriarch's concept of God was complicating his problems (Job 38). Job had thought that God should come

running when he called. God revealed more of his greatness to Job, and then Job saw more clearly his position as
a finite creature in relation to his infinite creator (Job
42:2–6). One explanation for God's silence is that God may
have reasons for not responding to our prayers of which we
may be totally ignorant (see Job 1–2). This is one of the
most important revelations about prayer in Scripture. It is
interesting that God revealed it so early in human history,
yet most people struggle to learn it. A proper biblical understanding of God will obviate many of our problems about
why God responds to prayers as he does.

During this historical period, most biblical prayers
requested things from God. Many were personal petitions,
such as Abram's prayer for a son and Eliezer's prayer for
guidance in his search for Isaac's bride. This type of prayer
is especially prominent in the record of Jacob's life, probably because Jacob was a grasper. He wanted many things
for himself.

Intercession was also common among the patriarchs.
Abram interceded for Ishmael (Gen. 17:20), the righteous
in Sodom (Gen. 18:23–33), and Abimelech (Gen. 20:17).
Isaac entreated Yahweh for Rebekah (Gen. 25:21), and Job
prayed for his friends (Job 42:10). Melchizedek blessed
Abram (Gen. 14:19), and Jacob blessed his many sons (Gen.
48:15, 20; 49:28), while Noah blessed Japheth and cursed
Canaan (Gen. 9:25–27).

Besides prayers for action, we note several prayers of
inquiry (e.g., Gen. 15:1–9). Job's prayers were mainly
prayers of inquiry.

On what basis did people appeal to God in prayer during this period? It was because God is who he is. People
prayed to God because he had revealed that he had an interest in them and that he was a person they could approach.
His promises to Abraham and his descendants in the Abra-

hamic covenant gave people ground on which to appeal to him and to expect from him (Gen. 17:20; 25:21; 32:9–12; 48:15, 20; 49:28). God also gave other promises to humankind and to individuals that encouraged them to pray (e.g., Gen. 3:14–19; 9:15).

One example of prayer based on God's interest in people simply as his creatures is Abimelech's prayer in Genesis 20:4. This Gentile king appealed to God's justice when he asked God to treat him consistent with his righteous behavior (Gen. 18:23–33). Gentiles at this time apparently had no special promises to claim so they appealed to God as their Creator.

There are more prayers based on God's making himself known in this period of history than in any other. In these introductory books of the Bible there is a concentration of revelation about the person of God. Abraham based his vow that he would take no reward from the four pagan kings on God's previous revelation of himself as El Elyon, the most high God (Gen. 14:18, 22). He believed that such a God would fulfill his promises and would provide for him. Hagar based her prayer of praise on God's self-revelation as the God who sees, El Roi (16:13). Abram worshiped God in response to his revelation as El Shaddai, God Almighty (Gen. 17:2–3), and he interceded for Sodom with the "Judge of all the earth" (Gen. 18:25). Abraham called on the name of Yahweh El Olam, the everlasting God, in prayer after God had revealed himself as such (Gen. 21:33). When God provided a ram in the place of Isaac, Abraham called on Yahweh Jireh as he offered the animal as a sacrifice in his son's place (Gen. 22:14). In all these cases, the name of God represented the revelation of the person of God. As God revealed his person and character more fully, people continued to approach him in prayer more intelligently. Similarly, the more we know about another human being we are addressing the better we can converse with and appeal to that person.

People characteristically prayed to God by direct conversation during this time. They talked as freely and familiarly with God as if he were standing in front of them (Gen. 3:9–13; 15:1–9). This was especially true during humankind's earliest history. In some cases they did speak face to face with God, when he came to them as the Angel of Yahweh (Gen. 16:7–12; 18:22). In these dialogues, God drew near to people and they drew near to him. Sometimes the bold approach of these early saints seems almost naive in the light of later revelations of God's greatness and glory. Nevertheless God welcomed them because he desires our fellowship and delights to bless us.

To summarize the revelation about prayer during the pre-Mosaic period we may point out four characteristics. First, God spoke to people more than people spoke to God. At least this is the emphasis of Scripture. The record of Noah's life is a good example. Noah received much revelation from God, but his only recorded words to God are a brief prophetic doxology, benediction, and imprecation (Gen. 9:25–27).

Second, God spoke more directly to people during this period than he did later. Consequently, people's responses to God in prayer were generally naive, familiar, and direct. Their prayers resemble simple, childlike talk dealing with the basic necessities and sometimes trivial incidents of life.

Third, prayer and sacrifice often went together at this time. Early man seems to have wanted to bolster his petition with a gift to God. This characteristic is especially clear in the vow passages such as Jacob's bargain with God (Gen. 28:20–22). However, sacrificing also contained the deeper implication of vicarious substitution that vowing did not (Gen. 22:13). From the fall humans sensed their need for something or someone that could atone for their sins. The sacrifices they offered to God expressed this need.

Fourth, God usually responded to people's prayers swiftly. Job's case is exceptional. This immediate response was doubtless a mark of prayers in this period because of the direct communication that many biblical characters enjoyed with God then. Rapid answers strengthened their faith. It was not as easy to believe God then as it is now, since people then did not have as full a revelation of God's person and program. We are greatly blessed to live when we can know God's complete revelation to humankind.

Prayer in Israel before the Monarchy

God's creation of the nation Israel begins a new chapter in his revelation. Many scholars view the exodus as the time Israel came into existence, whereas others believe the giving of the Mosaic law was the proper commencement of her national life. We shall include the early chapters of Exodus in this period, chapters that contain revelation about God forming the nation. The end of this period, for our purposes, will be the close of the judges' rule. Therefore we shall be looking into the revelation of prayer primarily in the books of Exodus through 1 Samuel 10.

We discover much new revelation about prayer as we read this part of biblical history. One of the outstanding new revelations has to be how patient God is with people who have weak faith, who find it difficult to trust him. God's early dealings with Moses clearly reveal this (Exod. 3:4–6:12). Moses had grown up to be very self-confident. He had a natural reason for feeling this way: he had all the privileges of aristocracy during the first forty years of his life. He enjoyed a secure environment, an excellent education, and opportunities to go to interesting places and to do important things.

Josephus wrote that he became a successful general in the Egyptian army. But when Moses sought to liberate his people in his own strength, he failed miserably. God taught Moses humility on the Midian desert for the next forty years of his life. When God called him to return to lead his people out of slavery, Moses had no self-confidence. Unfortunately, he did not have much God-confidence either. God proceeded to teach his servant that Yahweh was adequate to accomplish what Moses could not. Before then, however, God had to encourage Moses repeatedly to get him back to Egypt. The Lord rebuked Moses' weak faith (Exod. 4:14–17). Moses knew God well enough to have trusted and obeyed him more. Nevertheless God was patient with Moses' weak faith and gave him opportunities to strengthen his faith by trusting God.

God's deliverance of the Israelites from their Egyptian bondage precipitated the first public song of praise that the Bible records (Exod. 15:1–19). This "Song of the Sea" was the direct result of redemption. God's redemption of his people has been a major cause of thanksgiving and praises ever since that day (see Rev. 5:9–10).

Israel's war with the Amalekites teaches us the mighty effect of intercessory prayer (Exod. 17:12; cf. Num. 16:47–48). God's people had engaged a spiritual enemy, one that wanted to frustrate God's promises and purposes for his people. Almost all students of this passage have seen prayer in Moses' lifting up his hands to God, supported by Aaron and Hur. As their leader faithfully persevered in intercession, God blessed his people with victory over their spiritual enemy. When he grew tired and stopped praying, the enemy could advance. God's people were to learn by this experience that strength for victory over the ungodly powers of the world can come only through persistent intercession to God.

During this period God revealed that the ark of the covenant, specifically the mercy seat, the lid of the ark, had special significance in their communion with him (Exod. 25:22; cf. Num. 7:89). This was where God chose to abide among his people during their sojourn in the wilderness. Although Israelites could address God in prayer anywhere, it was at the ark that he dwelt in a particular local sense. Therefore the ark became a special place of prayer where Israel's high priest, acting as the people's representative, offered sacrifices and prayed for them. The first mention of incense, symbolic of prayer, occurs in this period (Exod. 30:1, 7–9; cf. Ps. 141:2; Luke 1:10; Rev. 5:8; 8:3). Incense continually ascended from the tabernacle before the very presence of God, picturing the constant prayers of his people heavenward.

Israel's apostasy involving the golden calf moved Moses to plead with God for his unfaithful people (Exod. 32:11–14). The people had broken the conditional Mosaic covenant and were therefore vulnerable to God's abandoning them. Moses pled with God not to forsake his people because it would result in the other nations thinking that Yahweh was unfaithful to his promises. The text records that God heeded Moses' petition and did not cast the people off. This prayer is an excellent example of prayer for the glory of God. In earlier prayers, the desire for God's honor is not as obvious (cf. Gen. 18:25). Here it was clearly the basis of Moses' urgent appeal to spare the nation. This is the highest level from which we can appeal to God in prayer. God's reputation should always be the primary concern of his people (Matt. 6:9; cf. 1 Cor. 10:31; Col. 3:17).

Following the incident of the golden calf Moses realized that he needed to know God much better if God was going to remain with his people and lead them into the Promised Land (Exod. 33:12–16). As Yahweh's vice-regent, Moses sensed his need to understand and communicate with his Master more effectively (cf. Phil. 3:10). Failure, like an alarm clock, often wakes us up to our need for a more intimate relationship with God. We observe throughout Scripture that the better someone knew God, as a result of appropriating what God had revealed about himself, the fewer problems that one had with prayer. Moses was a mighty intercessor. I once counted seventeen separate instances of his interceding for Israel that the divine Author has preserved for us in Scripture. When Moses got to know God better, he became a fervent intercessor because he learned that appealing to God in prayer is effective.

When Moses died, God shifted in his method of revealing his will slightly (Num. 27:21). God had frequently communicated with Moses face to face. Now he communicated his will primarily through the high priest's Urim and Thummim (see chap. 3), which he had used to a lesser degree during Moses' lifetime. The Urim and Thummim evidently became God's normal way of revealing his will and granting answers to prayer. Of course, he continued to speak directly to his prophets, and occasionally others, using visions, dreams, and direct revelations (Num. 12:6; 1 Sam. 3:4, 21; 16:12). However, answers for the nation normally came through the Urim and Thummim.

In the Mosaic covenant, God revealed that he would avenge his people (Deut. 32:35). This promise became the basis for imprecatory prayers in which believers called on him to take vengeance and execute justice (see Ps. 94:1–3). We find such prayers later in the Old Testament.

Hannah's prayer helps us understand that prayer is not synonymous with asking (1 Sam. 2:1–10). The biblical writer called what she said prayer, but her prayer did not contain any petition, only praise and thanksgiving. This is helpful to observe when we define prayer.

The outstanding prayers in both quantity and effectiveness during this epoch were prayers of intercession. Two of the greatest intercessors in the Bible were Moses and Samuel (Jer. 15:1). Moses "called aloud and earnestly" for God to remove the plague of frogs, for example (Exod. 8:12). His prayer for victory over Amalek was certainly one of the most powerful of all time (Exod. 17:12). He repeatedly interceded for Israel, asking God to spare the nation when in his wrath he would have abandoned it (Exod. 32:11–14; 31:34; Num. 14:13–19; Deut. 9:18–20, 25–29). Moses prayed whenever the ark departed from one place in its wilderness march and whenever it rested in another. He asked that God would scatter his enemies and return to the multitudes of his people (Num. 10:35–36).

Samuel was the last of Israel's judges and the first official prophet. The Bible calls Abraham and Moses prophets, but Samuel was the first in the order of the prophets that God raised up to receive and transmit his messages during Israel's monarchy. Samuel regarded praying for his nation as one of his primary duties as a prophet. He viewed failing to pray for the people as sin (1 Sam. 10:22). Thus we can see that Moses and Samuel, arguably the two greatest leaders of God's people during this period of biblical history, regarded praying for those under their care to be one of their primary leadership responsibilities (cf. Acts 6:1–4; 13:1–2; 1 Tim. 2:1–4).

Samuel interceded for his nation too, praying that Yahweh would save Israel from the powerful hand of the Philistines (1 Sam. 7:5–12). He prayed when the people prematurely insisted on appointing a king (1 Sam. 8:6). He prayed when Saul became king (1 Sam. 12). He also pled for Saul after God rejected him as Israel's monarch (1 Sam. 15:11, 35; 16:1).

Notable also during this era were the prayers of Israel's leaders for divine guidance as the nation anticipated, entered, and settled the Promised Land (Num. 27:5; Judg. 1:1; 1 Sam. 10:22).

On what bases did people approach God in prayer at this time? As in the earlier period, they prayed to him because of what they knew about him. The general knowledge of God that all people possess through nature and tradition led many people to pray. However, the biblical record of this period focuses on the Israelites primarily. They knew God better than the Gentiles because God gave unique revelations of himself to them. God revealed during this period that he had a special concern for people who were unusually dependent, such as widows (Exod. 22:23), the deprived (Exod. 22:27), and the poor (Deut. 24:15).

God had revealed to Abraham that he would use Israel to bring blessing to all humanity and that he would bless Israel particularly (Gen. 12:1–3; cf. Exod. 32:11–14; Deut. 9:27; 26:13–15). Consequently, many prayers in this period called upon God to honor what he had promised Abraham's descendants. Moses prayed that God would accompany his chosen people into the Promised Land, would pardon their sins, and would view them as his inheritance (Exod. 34:5–9). He asked that God would identify Israel with himself and bless the people (Num. 6:23–27). He appealed to God's honor and to his grace in view of these promises (Num. 16:22; Exod. 32:31–32).

God also promised Moses and the Israelites at Mount Sinai that he would bless Israel greatly if they obeyed him faithfully. If they did not, however, they could expect chastening and discipline. God would never abandon them completely, but they would fail to enjoy the fullness of his blessing if they departed from him. The Mosaic covenant was an agreement between Yahweh and Israel in which Yahweh, Israel's King, agreed to certain blessings for the Israelites, his servants, contingent on their trust and obedience. God brought this covenant in alongside the Abrahamic covenant to clarify for the Israelites how they could maximize the benefits promised in the Abrahamic covenant (Gal. 3). There are also many specific promises in the Mosaic covenant to which we find reference in the prayers of the Israelites following its ratification.

As in the previous period, people who received special revelations from God often responded by addressing God in prayer directly. Moses and God spoke face to face (Exod. 33:11; Deut. 34:10). Joshua and Samuel also spoke to God directly, but they seem to have had fewer theophanies than Moses did (Num. 27:21; Judg. 1:1; 1 Sam. 3:4; 16:12). Thus it became increasingly common for people to pray as we do today, without any visible representation of God when they addressed him.

Reference to the common posture of praying with hands uplifted to heaven appears first at this time (Exod. 17:12). Praying near the localized presence of God became popular too (Exod. 25:22; Num. 7:89; 1 Sam. 1:3). Even today pious Jews prefer to pray at the Wailing Wall in Jerusalem because it is the site available to them that is closest to the ancient Holy of Holies. The older idea of praying on a hilltop to get close to heaven was refined in Israel with God's appearance over the ark. After Yahweh's descent on the completed tabernacle, the Israelites wanted to get as close to the ark as possible to pray.

Boldness in prayer characterizes this early period of Israel's history (Exod. 32:31–32; 33:12–16). However, the Mosaic law brought increasing revelation about the holiness of Yahweh and the sinfulness of humans. This made people more fearful of approaching God in prayer than was true earlier. Nevertheless there are still many instances of people boldly approaching God in prayer, particularly people who understood God, such as Moses and Samuel. Moses went as far as offering his own life for the nation that he loved (Exod. 32:31–32).

The introduction of the Levitical system of worship brought increased mediation into prayer. The Israelites learned that as sinners they could not approach a holy God without proper mediation and that God set the standards. The priests represented the interests of the people to God. They interceded daily for the nation. The prophets not only interceded for the people but also brought the words of God to them. The tabernacle structure and ritual helped the people learn about their proper relationship to Yahweh in worship.

It is noteworthy that, in contrast with later Rabbinic Judaism, the Mosaic law does not contain any specific instruction concerning prayer. Some scholars cite Deuteronomy 26:1–15 as an exception, but this instruction deals more with the attitude behind prayer than with prayer itself. Individuals could continue to pray to God anywhere and at any time, as they had previously. The Mosaic law, however, determined the whole system of worship in Israel, which included prayer. Evidently the Israelites did not need further instruction about private prayer. Prayer could be directly to God, but worship had to follow the specified guidelines. Perhaps God wanted the Israelites to express themselves spontaneously to him, since prayer offered only as a duty does not please him.

Prayer during the Monarchy

This era of biblical history extends from the reign of King Saul, Israel's first monarch, through the reign of King Zedekiah, the last Jewish king of the surviving kingdom of

Judah. This is a long period of history running from the eleventh to the sixth centuries B.C. The books of Samuel, Kings, and Chronicles are the major historical sources for this period. The pre-exilic prophets also contribute to our understanding of this time, and the Psalms give us more insight.

There is not as much new revelation about prayer in this period as there was in the previous two. King David appointed several different groups of priests to carry out specialized duties connected with the worship of God, which included offering prayers (1 Chron. 16:4; 25:1–3; 2 Chron. 7:6–7; 29:28–30). Solomon dedicated his temple as a house of prayer, further ritualizing prayer (1 Kings 8; Isa. 56:7). King Hezekiah later organized the priests and Levites, resulting in even more formalization in national worship (2 Chron. 31:2). Prayer at fixed times for specific purposes became an even more settled tradition during this period (1 Chron. 23:30; 2 Chron. 2:4–6; Ps. 5; 55:17).

Prayer in the Psalter appears characteristically as the pouring out of one's heart to God (Ps. 42:4; 62:8; 142:2). Many different types of prayers appear in the Psalms including complaint, petition, intercession, confession, and imprecation. The Psalms often begin with lament and close with praise (Ps. 57:6–11; 69:30–36). This is the natural result of bringing one's concerns to God in prayer (Phil. 4:6–7). Some psalms contain group or national petitions; others voice personal concerns; still others combine both types. The Psalms teach us that people have prayed about many different situations and out of a wide variety of emotions. We should therefore never hesitate to take anything to God in prayer. The psalmists found relief in the practice of praying even when no answer was immediately forthcoming. Talking some situation over with God should give us even more satisfaction than discussing it with a human friend does.

Praise is the most common type of prayer in the Psalms. The psalmists praised or thanked God for something in almost every psalm. Imprecations, while not common, occur more in the Psalms than in any other book of the Bible (cf. Jer. 10:23–25; 18:19–23). In them the psalmists voiced their desire that God would vindicate himself and his people.

Intercessory prayers appear in this period mainly in the words of the prophets. Elijah's petitions are among the most well known because of God's striking answers.

Material, physical blessings rather than spiritual blessings were the common subjects of prayer during the monarchy. Although this holds true even for the Psalms, there are also outstanding prayers for spiritual needs in the Psalms. These needs are mainly communion with God and forgiveness of sins. Another striking feature of the prayers in the Psalms is their urgency (Ps. 28:1; 44:23).

We find few prayers based on God's general interest in people as his creatures in the divine record of Israel's monarchy. Most prayers appealed to God because of some special revelation that he had made earlier. The Israelites appealed to God increasingly because of his own character as added revelation helped them know him better (2 Sam. 6:18; 2 Kings 2:24; Ps. 9; 25; 54). The prophets helped the people appreciate their God by clarifying his relationship to them as well as by expounding his attributes. For example, they spoke of him as the Father of their nation (Isa. 63:16; 64:8; Jer. 3:4–5).

Appeals to God that reminded him of his promises to Abraham continued. God gave David further revelation about the seed aspect of his promise to Abraham (2 Sam. 7). From then on those promises formed an additional basis of appeal to God in prayer (2 Sam. 7:18–29; 2 Chron. 1:8–10; Ps. 89:38–51).

There are many prayers based on the promises in the Mosaic covenant in this era. These include promises of success in battle (1 Sam. 23:2), long life for the godly (e.g., 2 Kings 20:3), and physical prosperity for righteous conduct (Ps. 58:10–11; 118:25). Solomon counted on God's promise to bless his people if they sought him wholeheartedly (1 Kings 9:3; 2 Chron. 7:14–15). Elijah based his prayers on the promises that God had given. For example, God had promised that he would withhold rain from the land if his people departed from him and would bless them with rain if they returned to him (1 Kings 17–18).

In some of the psalms the writer based his request on his own righteousness and asked God to grant his petition because he had behaved better than his enemies (Ps. 35:13–16; 68:7–11). However, the psalmist was not claiming sinlessness (Ps. 69:5) but righteousness (Ps. 69:7–9). Frequently this claim to righteousness connects with a profession of trust in the Lord (Ps. 38:15; 71:5, 14). This trust was the reason the psalmist was righteous and could ask God to execute justice and to punish the wicked as he did.

During this period God revealed his will, including answers to prayer, through the high priest and through prophets to whom he gave dreams and visions. Israel's kings sought answers from both sources (1 Kings 22:15; Mic. 3:11). Both priests and prophets also interceded for the people, for they stood in favored positions before God that enabled them to do so. Moreover, as the Holy Spirit inspired them in their proclaiming of God's words, so he also inspired them to pray for God's concerns (cf. Rom. 8:26). David was both a king and a prophet. Thus we find him doing some things that prophets normally did while at other times he served as a king.

David, Elijah, and Jeremiah were all powerful intercessors. The divine record of Jeremiah's life teaches the importance of persistence and fervency in prayer (Jer. 7:27; 10:21–25; 11:14; 12:1–4; 14:11–12, 19–22; 15:1; 20; 33:3; 42:4).

There is much emphasis on the importance of repentance in this period, mainly in the prophets' writings. Spiritual decline during the monarchy followed the formalization of worship including ritual prayer. While the nation as a whole went down spiritually, this period of Israel's history produced many outstanding individuals who were men and women of prayer. Their relationship to God was vital, and their prayer lives testified to the reality of their relationship with God.

Prayer in the Exilic and Postexilic Period

The books that tell us about prayer during the exile are some portions of Jeremiah plus Ezekiel and Daniel. There is no mention of prayer in Esther, although there is one reference to fasting (Esther 4:16). Lamentations is one long lament concerning the destruction of Jerusalem. It contains many prayers for God to have mercy on his disobedient people and to remember his promises to the patriarchs.

The books that record Israel's return from exile and her reestablishment in the land are Ezra and Nehemiah plus the postexilic prophets: Haggai, Zechariah, and Malachi. Zechariah gives us little information about conditions during this period, for the book deals mainly with the future.

Sacrificing ceased with the destruction of Solomon's temple in 586 B.C. The Jews who went into captivity and those who remained in the land were not able to worship according to the Mosaic law because they had no authorized place of worship. Nonetheless they continued to pray (Dan. 6:10–11). The prophets encouraged the people to turn to the Lord in repentance and prayer (Jer. 31:33; 50:5). When they did return to the land, public prayer and singing played a prominent part in reestablishing national worship (Ezra 3:11). The builders prayed as they rebuilt the wall around Jerusalem (Neh. 2:4; 6:14; 13:22). Finally, they dedicated the fruits of their labor to the Lord with prayer (Neh. 12:40–42).

Prayers of confession mark this period of Israel's history. The Bible gives much attention to Daniel's and Nehemiah's private prayers of confession for their nation (Dan. 9:3–19; Neh. 1:4–11). Ezra and Nehemiah both led the restoration community in public confession (Ezra 9:5–15; Neh. 9:5–38). Clearly the people and their leaders realized that the captivity was Yahweh's punishment for their sins as a nation.

The person and character of God were prominent bases for these prayers (Neh. 9:5–38; Dan. 4:34). Those praying likewise appealed to the promises in the Abrahamic covenant (Ezra 7:27–28; 9:5–15; Dan. 2:20–23). The promises to forgive the truly penitent in the Mosaic covenant also were a basis for appeal to God (Neh. 1:4–11).

Even though the Israelites realized that their sins had driven them out of the land, and even though their leaders confessed their sins, they did not call on the Lord much themselves. They continued in apostasy (Isa. 43:21–22; Jer. 44:15–19; Ezek. 4:14; 9:8; 11:13; 20:49). Toward the end of the captivity, however, their hearts did turn back to the Lord (Ps. 106; Dan. 9:3–19).

After returning to the land, the people made a good start toward repentance and loudly confessed their guilt with vocal "amens" to the prayers of their leaders (Neh. 5:13; 8:6). Nevertheless it was not long before the majority had backslidden and were only going through the motions of praying and worshiping (Mal. 1:2, 6–7, 13, 17; 2:17; 3:7–8).

A minority of the people did fear God, however, and he paid attention to their prayers (Mal. 3:16).

The ejaculatory prayers of Nehemiah, who prayed as he worked, are notable because they show the proper attitude toward God amid daily circumstances (Neh. 5:19; 13:14, 22, 29, 31). Nehemiah cried out to God whenever a crisis arose (Neh. 4:4–5; 6:9, 14). He did not stop what he was doing but prayed while he worked (Neh. 2:4; 4:9). Prayer also played a prominent role in the lives of Israel's other leaders in this period: Ezekiel, Daniel, and Ezra. The prayers of these men in Scripture show how important a place prayer came to occupy in individual lives because of the exile.

Ephesians 3:14–19

For this reason I kneel before the Father, from whom his whole family in heaven and on earth derives its name. I pray that out of his glorious riches he may strengthen you with power through his Spirit in your inner being, so that Christ may dwell in your hearts through faith. And I pray that you, being rooted and established in love, may have power, together with all the saints, to grasp how wide and long and high and deep is the love of Christ, and to know this love that surpasses knowledge—that you may be filled to the measure of all the fullness of God.

5

Prayer in the New Testament

In one sense, the Old Testament doctrine of prayer ends with the end of the Old Testament. In another sense, it continues into the period of the life of Christ since he lived under the laws that governed Israel. Prayer as people practiced it during Jesus' day was an extension of Old Testament practices. Thus prayer in the messianic period reflects what existed in Israel under Mosaic law about four hundred years after the return from exile.

Prayer during the Life of Christ

This period contains more important advances in the progressive revelation of prayer than any other. Specifically it was Jesus' teaching about prayer and his own prayer life that shed much new light on this subject. Jesus had more to say about prayer than did any other biblical character. We shall consider what Jesus taught on prayer by dividing his teaching according to the ways he communicated it. We shall look first at his personal example, then at his direct teachings on prayer, and finally at his indirect teachings on this subject. The Gospels are the main source of our information.

The Gospels do not record many of Jesus' prayers. In fact, if we read them all together, we could probably do so in less than ten minutes. The Gospel writers, however, described Jesus as a man who spent many extended periods of time in prayer. Perhaps we do not have many of his prayers because what he taught and exemplified are more important than the words that he used when he prayed to his Father. Jesus was not a hermit or a recluse. He did not retreat from society but lived an active and busy life in Israel. Prayer occupied a natural place in his life, one with which modern believers can identify fully.

Jesus made a habit of praying before important events in his life. These events included his baptism, which launched his public ministry (Luke 3:21). He prayed about the selection of his disciples (Luke 6:12–13), before his transfiguration (Luke 9:29), and before his crucifixion (Luke 22:39–46; John 17; cf. Heb. 5:7).

Jesus' example of praying in Gethsemane is particularly significant (Luke 22:39–46). As he anticipated his arrest, trials, and crucifixion, Jesus prepared himself by praying to his Father. He did so in part to avoid entering into temptation (Luke 22:46). The disciples did not sense their great need for God's help, so they slept. But Jesus anticipated conflict and prepared himself for it with prayer.

What Jesus prayed in Gethsemane is also important. As a man, he struggled with fulfilling the will of God. He prayed, "Father, if you are willing, take this cup from me; yet not my will, but yours be done" (Luke 22:42). There are several indications in the Gospels and elsewhere in the New Testament that when Jesus became a man he adopted the limitations common to humanity. He retained the nature of God, but he also adopted the nature of man. He restricted his physical presence to one location at a time, for example. He said that he did not know some things evidently because he chose to limit his omniscience during his incarnation (Matt. 24:36; cf. Phil. 2:6–7). Thus when Jesus prayed, he prayed as a man. Luke's Gospel, which stresses Jesus' humanity, records more of Jesus' prayer life than does any other Gospel.

Jesus made a request of his Father in Gethsemane. He asked that if it was the Father's will he would remove the cup from Jesus. The cup is a common Old Testament figure of divine judgment. The prophets announced that God would give the cup of his wrath to many of Israel's neighbor nations to drink. Jesus was asking to escape having to bear the punishment for the sins of mankind if it was God's will. However, he subsumed this desire under another one that was more important to him. He prayed primarily that God's will would be done.

This prayer is helpful to observe because we often do not know what God's will may involve. Is it God's will that Aunt Sally recover from her illness? Is it God's will that we travel to San Diego on Thursday? Jesus' pattern of prayer encourages us to present our preferences to God in prayer but to submit them to the will of God. Disciples of Jesus Christ should desire God's will above everything, even our personal preferences. Jesus expressed that priority by how he prayed in Gethsemane, and we should follow his example. When we know what the will of God is, we can pray confidently for it. When we do not know, we should pray subject to his will, as Jesus did.

Jesus' intercession for others is noteworthy too. He prayed for individuals such as Peter (Luke 22:32), the soldiers around his cross (Luke 23:34; cf. Isa. 53:1), and his present and future disciples (John 17:6–26). His intercessory ministry continues today (Rom. 8:34; Heb. 7:25). He prays from heaven for his own.

There are four primary sources of Jesus' teaching on prayer in the Gospel records: the Lord's Prayer, Jesus' parables, his upper-room discourse, and his high-priestly prayer. There is also incidental instruction about prayer.

The Lord's Prayer

Jesus evidently gave the teaching that we call the Lord's Prayer on two separate occasions. It is the "Lord's Prayer" in the sense that it came from him, not that he prayed it himself. The record in Matthew's Gospel occurs in the context of the Sermon on the Mount (Matt. 6:9–13). In this sermon, Jesus taught his disciples how to live. Jesus repeated his teaching on prayer, with minor variations, in response to a question that his disciples asked him after he finished praying privately (Luke 11:2–4). On both occasions he taught disciples (Matt. 5:1; Luke 11:1), people who were interested in learning from him as an authoritative teacher. Some of them may have already come to believe that he was the God-man, while others, including Judas Iscariot, had not yet reached that conclusion. Thus his teaching was not limited to believers, although it was clearly intended for those who did and would believe on him. The repetition of this teaching in Scripture indicates its great importance.

Jesus introduced his teaching in two different ways. In the Sermon on the Mount he told his disciple to pray "in this way" (Matt. 6:9), whereas on the occasion that Luke recorded he said, "When you pray, say . . ." Thus Jesus intended what he taught as a model for his disciples' prayers and as a prayer that they could repeat, a model prayer. He did not limit their praying to these words, but he gave them guidance in praying.

Perhaps the most important thing that Jesus taught in the Lord's Prayer was what he said first. Jesus said that his disciples should think of God as their heavenly Father when they come to him in prayer. As I have mentioned before, the way a person thinks about God will affect how he or she prays.

The idea that God is the personal Father of individual believers was a new one when Jesus first introduced it. The Old Testament spoke of God as the Father of the nation of Israel collectively, but it never referred to him as the Father of individual Israelites. There is no record that the rabbis of Jesus' day taught this view of God. Consequently, this idea probably shocked Jesus' hearers. It probably seemed too familiar to address God as one's Father. But that is how Jesus taught us to think of God when we approach him in prayer, as a loving Father who is in heaven. He has none of the imperfections of earthly fathers. He is what every father should be, the ideal father who is in heaven.

It is possible to think of God in any number of ways when we pray. He is, after all, the sovereign King of the Universe, the almighty God, the eternal God, the covenant-keeping God, the victorious Warrior. Certainly it is appropriate to think of God in all these roles, as he has revealed himself in these terms. Nevertheless, when Jesus' disciples come to God in prayer it will be most appropriate and helpful for us to think of him as our heavenly Father. Why? Because that will determine to some extent how we pray and what we pray. It should make us speak freely with God and be honest with him. Since he is God, our *heavenly* Father, we need to give him proper respect (see Eccles. 5:2). From the Oriental viewpoint, which was characteristic of Jesus' culture, the father in the family deserved great respect and admiration. A good son was a son who patterned his life after his father's example and followed in his father's footsteps. Thinking of God as our heavenly Father will obviate many of our problems in prayer.

Jesus then proceeded to teach his disciples to pray for six things. In Luke's account, he, or Luke, condensed his former teaching somewhat. The first three petitions deal with God's needs and the last three with the needs of disciples. This indicates that our concern in prayer should be primarily what is most important to God and secondarily what we need. A devoted son and disciple should put his Father's interests first. This order gives us an insight into the purpose of prayer. It is not primarily to get things for ourselves but to advance the glory and plan of God.

The first petition requests that God's name be hallowed. The name of God represents everything about him; it is equivalent to his reputation. When we pray for this, we are praying that everyone including ourselves will treat God as holy. Holy means different, specifically different from sinful humans. God is unique in his purity. His love is pure. His words are pure. His motives are pure. His character is pure. He is a person of complete integrity. When we pray that his name will be hallowed, we are asking that people will acknowledge him for who he is. One of our privileges as his disciples is to represent him to those who do not know him. Jesus taught here that one of our primary concerns should be that people get to know him as he really is. That is key to glorifying him and blessing them.

Jesus next taught us to pray that God's kingdom would come. God revealed much about his coming rule in the Old Testament. He promised that it would indeed come one day and that a descendant of David would rule the nations with an iron shepherd's rod. The iron rod symbolized absolute control by a good shepherd (Ps. 2). So in praying this second petition we are not praying that this kingdom will come as opposed to its not coming. God has promised that it will come. We are praying for it to come soon. We are expressing a longing for the coming of God's rule that will result in the vindication of our Savior and the balancing of the scales of justice. John the Baptist and Jesus came preaching that the kingdom promised in the Old Testament was at hand. When Jesus taught this prayer, it could have come very soon if the Israelites had accepted him as their Messiah. They did not. Consequently the kingdom still lies in the future. Jesus' disciples should look forward to its coming as John the Baptist and Jesus did and should pray for its arrival. The coming of that kingdom will be the best thing this world has ever seen. Therefore we can understand why Jesus taught us to keep its coming in the forefront of our thinking and praying.

The third petition, which Jesus omitted from his repetition of this teaching in Luke, deals with an aspect of the former request. When God's kingdom comes, his will will be done on earth as it is in heaven. Still we should not be content to sit back and pray for the kingdom to come. We should make the doing of God's will a particular concern of ours here and now as we anticipate the coming of the kingdom. Not only should we do God's will ourselves, but we should try to bring submission to God's authority into our world now. Praying for it reminds us that it can only be done as God gives grace and enablement. The will of God will not come only by legislation or social action. God must bring it to pass. This is why we need to make the doing of God's will here and now a primary subject of our praying.

The remaining three petitions deal with the primary personal needs of disciples. First, we need to petition God for our daily bread. This prayer reminds us that God is the provider of all the necessities of life. Bread often stands for basic needs in the Bible as it does in modern symbolism. When we speak of bread as the staff of life we are speaking of more than just flour kneaded and baked into loaves. We are using bread figuratively to represent the basic necessities of life (cf. Matt. 4:4). We are praying that God will provide us with the things we need to live and serve him as his disciples. Furthermore Jesus reminded us that we need these things day by day. We need to acknowledge that we truly live from hand to mouth since he provides us with these things. We are dependent on him daily for what we need, and we need to acknowledge our dependence on him in prayer. We need his provision this day and every day. We need him to provide our needs today and day by day.

Some Christians believe that asking for physical needs evidences lack of faith in God's love, faithfulness, and ability to provide. Making requests for these things seems to them to show a lack of faith rather than faith in God. However, Jesus Christ commanded us to ask God for what we need to carry out his will. Certainly God is loving, faithful, and able to provide without our asking him for anything. Nevertheless he has commanded us to ask him for what we need. If we never asked him for these things, we would forget that they come from him and that we are dependent on him for them. Praying for what we need is a discipline of dependence. It helps us keep ourselves and God in the proper perspective. He is the source of every good gift (James 1:17), and we are totally dependent on him to meet all our needs (John 15:5).

We need to request God's pardon as well as his provision because we sin daily. Debts (Gr. *opheilema*) are what we owe others, people and God, because we offend them (Matt. 6:11). Sins are all our offenses against God and others. Jesus, or Luke, used the general word for sins (Gr. *hamartias*) in Luke 11:4. The evidence that we realize our need for forgiveness is that we forgive others who owe us. Jesus expounded on the importance of forgiving others to secure divine forgiveness (Matt. 6:14–15). Our horizontal relationships need correcting before we can enjoy a clear vertical relationship with our heavenly Father.

The promises that God forgives the sins of all who trust in his Son—past, present, and future—do not contradict this teaching (Rom. 8:1). God forgives the guilt of our sins once for all. He will never condemn us for our sins. However, as forgiven sons of God, we can and do offend God with our sins, and this affects our daily fellowship with him. Therefore we need to confess our sins (1 John 1:9), not to make our salvation more secure but to restore our fellowship with God. Justification secures forensic or legal forgiveness, but confession secures family forgiveness. When we sin, God does not throw us out of his family, but our fellowship with him suffers, and that is why we need to confess our sins as believing disciples.

The sixth and final petition also may appear at first to involve a contradiction in biblical revelation. James wrote that God does not tempt anyone (James 1:13), but Jesus taught us to pray that he would not tempt us. The solution appears to be that Jesus was using another figure of speech, litotes, that asserts a positive idea by using its negative opposite. For example, the expression, "That's no big deal," means, "That is a small matter"; it is insignificant. "Lead us not into temptation" means, "Keep us away from temptation." God tempts no one, but he allows us to experience temptation from the world, the flesh, and the devil (Job 1–2; 1 John 2:15–17; Rom. 7:18–24; 1 Pet. 5:8). By praying this petition we express our felt need for God's protection from temptation that could come our way. It is a request that God would allow us to experience as little temptation as possible. It voices our need for God's help in avoiding and dealing with temptation.

Jesus' teaching in Matthew includes the other side of the coin, which Luke did not record. Deliverance from evil, or the evil one, either translation is legitimate, is what we need. Rather than entering temptation we ask for deliverance from it and the evil that it comes from and leads to.

The closing doxology in Matthew attributes the kingdom, power, and glory to God forever. There is some question about whether this statement was in the original autograph of Matthew's Gospel or whether a scribe added it later. I prefer to include it. In either case, it expresses a sentiment worthy of repetition.

The first three petitions address the person, the program, and the power of God. His interests should come first for his disciple sons. The second three deal with his provision, his pardon, and his protection. These requests represent our basic needs.

Jesus also taught his disciples three parables that deal with prayer.

Parables about Prayer

The Teaching about God's Desire to Bless

Jesus followed up his teaching in the Lord's Prayer, when he repeated it, with a parable and further instruction (Luke 11:5–13). The parable has often been called the parable of the persistent friend, but the real emphasis is on God's graciousness rather than on the friend's persistence. The parable appears in Luke 11:5–8, and the Lord's further teaching on prayer continues through verse 13.

The point of the parable is that persistence succeeds when friendship fails. Even though the friend would not get up and give his neighbor what he wanted because he was his friend, the neighbor's persistence moved his friend to grant his request (Luke 11:8). If we took the parable by itself, we might conclude that Jesus' point was that we can get things from God by prayer if we persist in asking him that he would not give us if we failed to persist. This is true; another parable taught the importance of persisting in prayer (Luke 18:1–8). But this parable's purpose is different. It sets the stage for the teaching that follows. In verses 9–13 we learn that while persistence is important we need to recognize something even more important when we pray. We need to understand that the heart of our heavenly Father is very different from the heart of the friend who finally conceded to his neighbor's request. As Jesus did so often in his parables, he taught here by contrasting people and their attitudes. Specifically he contrasted the reluctance of the friend with the readiness of the Father.

Verse 9 urges disciples of Jesus to keep on asking from our heavenly Father, to keep on seeking what we need from him, and to keep on knocking on heaven's door to obtain our needs (cf. vv. 3–4). The progression is from the less to the most desperate attitude in prayer. In each case, no matter how strongly we may sense our need for God's provision, Jesus promised that God would give what we request. He does not give only to those who knock long and loud. He also gives to those who keep asking. God's willingness to give us what we need is the point of this verse even more than the importance of our persisting in prayer.

In verse 10 Jesus restated this point, probably because it is so hard to believe. "Everyone," in the context of the Lord's Prayer (vv. 2–4), refers to disciples who ask God for things that will glorify him, advance his will, and enable them to serve him. This verse is a strong encouragement to bother God with these requests. The friend who came knocking on his neighbor's door at midnight did not receive a warm reception. In contrast God will welcome anyone warmly who comes to him asking for the things that Jesus told disciples to pray for in the Lord's Prayer. No time is a bad time to make such a request. God does not go to sleep at night; he is always awake and available to help. His other responsibilities do not discourage him from responding to us when we ask; he is eager to help. We can count on getting what we need from him!

Jesus proceeded to illustrate how ready and willing God is to give these good gifts to disciples who ask him (vv. 11–12). Decent human fathers do not give their sons things that will harm them when they ask for things that they need. What father would substitute something that would disappoint and even endanger his son by substituting a snake or a scorpion, which resemble a fish and an egg? Good fathers don't do that kind of thing.

Jesus drew the conclusion to this lesson in verse 13. If human fathers will not give their sons what is a poor substitute for what they need, how much more will the heavenly Father give his sons only what is best for them! He may not give us what we think is best, but he will give us what he knows is best for us.

When Jesus gave this teaching, the gift of the Holy Spirit was the best gift that God gave people. He gave it only selectively in the Old Testament; few believers possessed the indwelling Spirit (cf. John 14:17). To be empowered by God's Spirit was the greatest blessing a Jew in Jesus' day could experience. Here Jesus used the Holy Spirit to represent the best gift that God can give one of his children. In our day, when the Holy Spirit indwells every believer (Rom. 8:9), we do not need to ask God for his Spirit. It was appropriate for Peter, James, and John to ask for the Spirit before Pentecost, but we do not need to request the Spirit. We do not need more of him since we have him in his fullness; he needs to have full control of us (Rom. 6:13; 12:1–2; Gal. 5:16).

This revelation should convince any disciple of Jesus Christ that when we come to our heavenly Father in prayer requesting the things that Jesus taught us to pray for, he will give them. We may have to keep on asking, seeking, and knocking for some time, but God will definitely provide our needs. We can count on this because of the character of our God. He is not just a good friend, as the neighbor in the parable was. He is our Father. He does not behave even as a good earthly father does. He behaves as a perfect divine Father does.

This teaching on prayer is foundational for disciples of Jesus Christ, those called into God's family and sent out on a divine mission (Matt. 28:19–20). It assures us that God will indeed provide all that we need to fulfill the calling that he has graciously given us (Matt. 28:19–20).

Jesus' Encouragement to Pray

Jesus told his disciples in the preceding teaching that they might have to wait a while before God gave them what they requested in prayer (Luke 11:9). Since answers to prayer are not always immediately forthcoming, we tend to get discouraged and to wonder if they will ever come. Jesus gave the parable in Luke 18:1–8 to encourage disciples of his always to pray and not to lose heart (v. 1).

In the previous teaching, Jesus contrasted our heavenly Father with a friend (Luke 11:5–8) and with an earthly father (Luke 11:11–12). In this one, he contrasted the heavenly Judge with an earthly judge. Formerly the emphasis was on giving out of love. Here it is on giving out of justice.

The judge in the parable was everything a judge in Israel was not supposed to be. He had no fear of God, and he did not respect people in need of justice. He was calloused to the pleas of a widow who in Jesus' day would have been without an advocate and destitute, and he was selfish. The only reason he finally gave in to the widow's constant requesting was that she wore him out.

Jesus contrasted God, the righteous Judge, with this wicked judge in verse 7. This wicked judge had only limited powers in one city, but God is the Judge of all humanity. The judge in the parable reluctantly dispensed justice because he was wicked, but God will judge fairly because he is a righteous Judge. The wicked judge gave justice to someone for whom he had no special regard, but God will give justice to those whom he has chosen to be his children. If the persistent pleas of a nameless widow moved this heartless judge, how much more will the persistent prayers of God's elect move him? If the wicked judge responded fairly soon because of the widow's persistence, how much more quickly will God respond to the persistent cries of his elect?

Jesus concluded his teaching by assuring his disciples that God would produce justice for them speedily (v. 8). As we go out into the world as ambassadors of Christ, we frequently receive unjust treatment from the nonelect. We call out to God to give us justice and to keep the enemy from triumphing over us. Jesus promised that God will give justice to his elect speedily.

But what about the Christian martyrs who have died unjustly? God does not seem to have produced justice speedily for them. Probably the solution lies in how we interpret the relative term *speedily*. This teaching on prayer lies in a context dealing with the Lord's return at the end of the age (Luke 17:37; 18:8b). In the light of Jesus' revelations about the future, one lifetime is not very long. Speedily does not necessarily mean during one's lifetime. As Peter later wrote, "One day is with the Lord as a thousand years and a thousand years as one day" (2 Pet. 3:8 KJV).

The end of verse 8 refers again to the Lord's return (cf. Luke 17:37). There will be few believers alive on the earth when he returns; there will not be much faith on the earth then. However, our faith can be seen in our praying. Persistence in prayer, which Jesus urged in this parable, demonstrates faith in God. Therefore as the end times approach, we should continue to pray persistently and not lose heart (v. 1) in spite of the injustice we may experience. Jesus here exhorted his disciples to remain faithful in prayer as the end approaches. God is a righteous, compassionate Judge who will give justice to his vulnerable and needy elect speedily, even though that justice may come after we die (see Rev. 6:10; 19:2).

Jesus' Teaching about Humility

Another parable follows the one we have just considered in Luke's Gospel (18:9–14). The second one followed the first chronologically, and they also connect because both deal with prayer. This parable of the Pharisee and the tax collector teaches that we should humble ourselves when we come to God, specifically in prayer.

The Pharisee was proud of himself and his righteous deeds. He assumed that God as well as other people would view him favorably because of his actions. The publican, or tax collector, did not cite anything about himself as a reason God should hear and answer his prayer. He cast himself on God's mercy, trusting in God for pardon rather than trusting in himself. Jesus explained that the tax collector's attitude is the one that God honors, not the Pharisee's. God justifies, declares righteous, those who trust in his mercy rather than those who declare themselves righteous.

The same attitude must be present in Jesus' disciples when we pray. We must cast ourselves on the mercy of God and not demand that he acknowledge us because of what we have done. By humbling ourselves we place ourselves in a position for God to exalt us (cf. James 4:10; 1 Pet. 5:6). The humble Christian will pray; the proud Christian will not. Notice that the Pharisee made no request of God. Prayer for him was a way to demonstrate his pious behavior, not a way to secure God's help. This parable teaches the importance of a right attitude in prayer, an attitude of dependence.

The Upper-Room Discourse

Just before his betrayal, arrest, and crucifixion, Jesus met with his disciples in an upper room to prepare them for what lay ahead of them. As they reclined around a table late that night, Jesus taught them many things (John 14–16). All of what he said prepared them for the time when he would be absent from them in heaven and they would be carrying out his mission for them on the earth. Part of what he taught them concerned their praying.

Jesus told the disciples that they should ask of their heavenly Father on the authority of Jesus Christ himself. God would give them what they asked of him when they prayed "in my name," Jesus said (John 14:13, 14; 15:16; 16:23–24). The apostle John picked up the importance of praying in Jesus' name and clarified in his first epistle what Jesus meant (1 John 5:14–15). Asking in Jesus' name means asking according to God's will. It means asking for things that we know are God's will or asking subject to God's will (cf. Luke 22:42). Praying in Jesus' name does not mean ending our prayers, ". . . in Jesus' name, amen." It means praying on the basis of Jesus Christ's person and work.

Recently a man who attends the same church I do told me that he was looking for a job as a computer programmer. I have another friend who was hiring people as programmers, so I encouraged this person to contact him. I said, "Feel free to use my name when you talk to him." The man did, and he got the job. Similarly, when we come into God the Father's presence and mention that we are there because of what his Son means to us, we get results.

If you have ever used a credit card you can appreciate what it means to pray in Jesus' name. When we offer payment with a credit card, it is the name on the card that makes all the difference. It acts as a password to secure what we request. If a friend gives you a check for your birthday, you can go to the bank and withdraw however much your benefactor has specified. It is his or her name that makes all the difference, not yours. Likewise Jesus has made the Father's resources available to us as disciples, and he has specified the conditions whereby we can tap into his limitless bounty.

Jesus promised his disciples that if they asked him for anything that was in harmony with God's will he would give it to them. The purpose of the asking and the answering is that the Father might receive glory (John 14:13). Jesus repeated the promise for emphasis several times (John 14:14; 15:16; 16:23–24). The results would be abiding fruit (John 15:16) and fullness of joy for the disciples (John 16:24).

The additional promise in John 15:7 guarantees that abiding disciples will get whatever they request in prayer. The key to this promise is the word *abide.* As Jesus and John used this term, they meant disciples who not only believed in Jesus but also walked in fellowship with him (cf. 1 John 1:1–4). Not every Christian's desires harmonize with God's. Sometimes we request things so we may consume them on our own lusts, not that we may carry out God's will (James 4:3). But when we are walking with the Lord and seeking to do his will, we will ask for what harmonizes with his will and what is for his glory. Those are the requests that he promised to grant.

Jesus referred to prayer toward the beginning, in the middle, and toward the end of this discourse. This shows how important prayer is to the disciples' mission in the interadvent age. Jesus spoke of the disciples' praying to him and to the Father. Either person is a legitimate one to address in prayer. However, since the Son glorifies the Father in the Trinity, it is more appropriate to address our prayers to the Father in the name of the Son and with the enablement of the Spirit.

Jesus' High-Priestly Prayer

Jesus' prayer in John 17 is his longest prayer that the Gospel evangelists recorded. It plays an important role in the fourth Gospel. In the Old Testament, prayers often accompanied farewell discourses that important individuals uttered under divine inspiration (cf. Gen. 49; Deut. 32–33). This one concluded Jesus' farewell upper-room discourse (John 14–16). The theme of the prayer is the glory of God and the disciples' good. The disciples' mission was prominently in Jesus' thoughts; this is what Jesus prayed about. This prayer is a foretaste of his present intercessory ministry. In view of John 18:1 it seems likely that Jesus prayed this prayer before he entered Gethsemane, either in the upper room or somewhere else in or near Jerusalem.

In the first five verses Jesus voiced requests for himself. His great passion was to glorify his Father. That should also be the driving desire of his disciples. As that desire directed Jesus' prayer here, so it should direct our praying. Jesus requested his own glorification only as a means to the end of the Father's ultimate glorification.

Jesus' glorification depended on the well-being of those whom the Father had given to him, his disciples. Therefore Jesus prayed for them too (vv. 6–19). The length of this section suggests that Jesus' concern for his disciples was greater than his concern for himself (cf. Luke 6:12; John 6:15; Luke 22:32; Rom. 8:34; Heb. 7:25). It was God's keeping power rather than the disciples' strength that made

Jesus confident as he prayed for them. Jesus based his requests on the fact that God had chosen the disciples out of the world and they belonged to God. He prayed specially for those who had believed on him. They stood in a special relationship to him. They needed special help from the Father because Jesus was about to leave them. Then Jesus prayed for their safety (vv. 11b–16) and their sanctification (vv. 17–19). These concerns undoubtedly remain prominent in Jesus' praying for his own now.

The remainder to the prayer contains Jesus' requests for future believers (vv. 20–26). These are those who would come to believe on him because the first generation of disciples witnessed. He requested unity (vv. 20–23) and glorification (vv. 24–26) for them. The whole prayer is a great revelation of the Savior's heart for his own. It also serves as a model for Christians in our intercession for one another and for those who will trust Jesus Christ in the future.

Other Instruction about Prayer from Jesus

Elsewhere in the Gospels we have other information that Jesus gave his disciples about conditions for effective prayer. We need to pray in faith, believing that God can answer our prayers (Mark 5:25–34; 7:24–30). He charged his disciples to ask God to thrust laborers out into the harvest fields (Matt. 9:38). He urged fervency in prayer (Matt. 26:36–39). He also repeated some themes during his ministry that I have already dealt with.

The people who besought Jesus for various reasons during his earthly ministry did not thereby pray to God in the customary sense. However, their petitions and words often illustrated various aspects of prayer. A condition that Jesus imposed for granting their requests was their belief that he could meet their need (Matt. 8:1–4; Mark 4:35–41). If they did not believe that, he sometimes rebuked them for lack of faith. Praying in faith therefore must mean praying with faith that God *can* do what we request. It does not mean believing that he *will* do what we ask, unless, of course, he has specifically promised to do what we are asking. Praying in faith does not mean convincing ourselves that what we pray will happen. It means that we believe that God can do what we request if that is his will.

God delayed some answers to requests to test the character and to increase the persistence of the persons praying (Mark 7:23). This appears to have been a method for stretching one's faith that God has used throughout history (cf. Job). The granting of any prayer request ultimately depends on the sovereign will of God (Matt. 20:22). This does not mean that God's actions are entirely unpredictable. He has revealed in Scripture what he will do and will not do in many instances. Therefore it is important to pray in harmony with the revealed will of God to get answers to our prayers.

Prayer in the Church

For the purposes of this study, I am using the term *church* to describe a historical period beginning with Jesus' ascension into heaven and ending with the consummation of the present age. All the New Testament books describe this period, but the Gospels and the Book of Revelation deal mainly with what immediately preceded it and what will follow it. There is quite a bit of new revelation in this period. I shall break it down according to the persons through whom God revealed it to us.

Luke

Luke gave us invaluable insight into the life of the early church. In Acts we see the disciples giving prayer a prominent place in their personal and corporate lives. The early Christians expressed the great dependence on God that they felt by praying frequently and fervently. The apostles considered prayer one of their primary duties along with the ministry of the Word (Acts 6:1–4). It was as the believers in Antioch of Syria were praying and fasting that God directed them to send Barnabas and Paul farther west into the Roman Empire. The missionaries prayed before they appointed elders in the new churches that they established. They realized the need for God's guidance and enablement for these new leaders. The church's expansion from Jerusalem to the uttermost parts of the earth was a result of prayer. The apostles obtained strength and encouragement from God in prison through prayer many times.

Paul

Next to Jesus Christ, the apostle Paul had more to say about prayer than did any other biblical character. Paul referred to prayer many times in the epistles that he wrote during his missionary journeys. One of his most important contributions to the doctrine of prayer was his teaching that the Holy Spirit cooperates in believers' prayers (Rom. 8:15, 26; Eph. 6:18). Christians are able to call God our Father because he has adopted us as his children. The evidence of this is our possession of and guidance by the Spirit of God (Rom. 8:14–15; Gal. 4:6; Eph. 1:13). The Holy Spirit helps us because we do not always pray for what is necessary. We sometimes pray only for what we think is important. The Holy Spirit himself helps us to recognize and to compensate for these deficiencies in our praying. He also intercedes for us in a way that we could not whenever we need this ministry. He does this by communicating the deepest groanings of our hearts that we cannot even express in words to God. He turns these unutterable desires into intercession in a manner that God hears. When we cannot express our deepest desires and feelings, the Spirit communicates these and offers them to God for us (Rom 8:26–27; cf. 2 Cor. 5:2–5).

The apostle Paul, as did Jesus Christ, testified to the importance of prayer not only by what he said about it but also by his example of praying. He was constantly praying for the people whom he evangelized and to whom he ministered. He requested the prayers of the saints to whom he sent his epistles, and he reported that his fellow workers joined him in praying for them. This aspect of his prayer concern comes through especially in his prison Epistles (Ephesians, Philippians, Colossians, and Philemon). Clearly Paul believed that the success of his labors depended on God's enablement and blessing that came in answer to prayer.

In his pastoral Epistles (1 and 2 Timothy and Titus) Paul urged that prayer be given a major place in the meetings of the churches and that the men should take the lead in praying (1 Tim. 2). He also recorded instructions for praying in public. The principle behind effective public praying is that these prayers should be orderly and edifying (1 Cor. 11:4–15; 14:14–17, 28). These prayers should reflect the order in nature, in the family, in government, and in society in general, and people leading in prayer should offer them appropriately. They should edify those who silently follow the person leading in prayer.

The Writer of Hebrews

This writer stressed the access that believers now have for entering God's presence in prayer through Jesus Christ. This access is the result of three things. First, we live under a new and better covenant, the new as compared to the old Mosaic covenant. Second, a new and better sacrifice has opened the way into God's presence, namely, Jesus Christ rather than animals. Third, we have a new and better high priest, Jesus Christ, who serves in a superior order, the order of Melchizedek as contrasted with Aaron's order. Jesus Christ ever lives to make intercession for believers (Heb. 7:25; 9:24), and he is our only Mediator now (Heb. 8:6; 9:15; 12:24; cf. 1 Tim. 2:5). We come into salvation only through Christ, and we come into God's presence in prayer only through him. Access in prayer follows access in salvation. Since the way is now open for all to come to God through the Savior, we should come confidently into God's presence to receive mercy and find grace to help in time of need (Heb. 4:16; 10:22).

James

The Epistle of James is an exposition of many themes from Jesus' Sermon on the Mount, with additional instruction. Since Jesus spoke of prayer in that sermon, it should be no surprise to find a strong emphasis on prayer in James's letter. James also dealt with practical issues involved in Christian growth, and prayer touches these frequently. James wrote of the need of faith when we pray (1:6–8), the problem of neglecting prayer, and the reasons some prayers go unanswered (4:2–3). His instruction about praying for the sick who suffer because of sin is unique (5:15). Prayer can have a significant role in removing this type of sickness, illness induced by sin, although, as the context clarifies, his prescription does not apply to all types of physical infirmity.

Christians who are ill because of sin in their lives should call for the elders of their church. It is interesting that James did not tell them to call for someone with the gift of healing. The elders should pray over the sick believer and anoint that person. The Greek word translated "anoint" refers to medicinal anointing rather than the type of anointing that was done in religious ceremonies. This procedure will be effective in restoring health only if it is God's will that the sufferer recover. However, the Lord will not withhold healing because of past sinning if the sick person confesses his or her sins. Therefore it is important that Christians confess their sins to one another as well as to God (cf. Matt. 6:14–15).

The illustration of Elijah's praying stresses the importance of praying and the powerful effect praying can have (James 5:17–18). The Greek text says that Elijah prayed praying. The point is that he prayed, not that he prayed fervently. James wanted his readers to appreciate the fact that prayer alone can accomplish mighty things. Therefore we should not neglect it in times of need. The power of prayer is that it secures the powerful working of God.

Peter

As we might expect, the apostle Peter's first epistle contains several references to prayer, since the epistle deals with how Christians are to live in a hostile world. There is thanksgiving for our hope as Christians (1 Pet. 1:3–12). Peter also warned us to remember that God is our judge to whom we must give an account of our lives (1 Pet. 1:17; 4:7). He warned husbands that failing to honor their wives could hinder their prayers (1 Pet. 3:7). Peter also viewed prayer as a resource for Christians who are suffering for their faith in Christ (1 Pet. 4:19; 5:7).

John

The apostle John's emphasis on prayer in his first epistle is similar to that of the writer of Hebrews. We may freely express anything that is on our hearts to God because we can draw near to God boldly. John also recorded clear promises guaranteeing answers to prayer (1 John 3:21–22; 5:14–15). The condition is asking in harmony with and subject to God's will (cf. John 14:13–14; 15:16; 16:23–24).

John's first epistle expounds many themes and uses many terms that Jesus referred to in the upper room discourse.

The prayer for the return of Jesus Christ that closes the Book of Revelation is also appropriate to the present age (Rev. 22:20). It is significant that this is the last prayer in Scripture. All prayer resolves itself at last into prayer for the Savior's coming. When he returns, all other desires of Jesus' faithful disciples will find fulfillment (cf. Matt. 6:10).

Jude

Jude viewed praying with the Holy Spirit's help as a way Christians should build ourselves up in our faith (Jude 20).

Summary of Prayers in the Church

We may summarize the content of prayers in the church age as follows. The early Christians prayed for boldness to witness (Acts 4:24–31), for God's blessings on fellow believers (Acts 1:2–3; 8:14–24; 19:6), and for divine guidance in important decisions (Acts 14:23). Their requests were for spiritual more than material blessings. Prayers of thanksgiving fill the biblical record of this period, especially in Paul's writings. He typically began his epistles by thanking God for something that he had done for his readers. He also reported to them what he was asking God to do for them, and he frequently requested their prayers for him and his work.

The basis of prayers in this period changed significantly. Instead of basing prayers on the character and covenant promises of God as revealed in the Old Testament, Christians base their prayers primarily on what Jesus Christ has done for them. Asking in the name of Jesus Christ becomes important in view of his person and his work on the cross (cf. Acts 3:16; 4:7, 10, 12, 17–18, 30). Jews and Gentiles

approach God in prayer on the same basis. This had not
been true earlier (Eph. 3:8; Col. 1:18–27). Formerly the
Israelites had offered prayer through the mediation of
human priests and prophets. Now the God-man in heaven
mediates the prayers of Christians (1 Tim. 2:5).

The writings of Paul best illustrate the method of praying in the present age. He not only exhorted prayer without ceasing (1 Thess. 5:17), but also practiced it. The scriptural record of his life indicates that Paul sensed his constant
and deep dependence on God, and this need led him to pray
without ceasing. Praying without ceasing does not mean
praying all the time. Obviously that would be impossible.
It means praying continually. The Greek word also
describes a hacking cough. A person with a hacking cough
cannot go for very long without coughing. Likewise the
Christian should not go for very long without praying. We
should pray about everything, and Paul did.

There are several notable characteristics of prayer in this
period of history. First, the early Christians addressed Jesus
Christ in prayer as well as God the Father (Acts 2:21, 36;
7:59; 9:5, 14, 21, 29; 22:16). However, it was customary
for them to address the Father primarily. Prayer in the name
of Jesus is the most outstanding characteristic of this present age.

Second, the indwelling ministry of the Holy Spirit, who
provides guidance and assistance in praying, is an important new characteristic. He enables believers to pray in the
will of God.

Third, prayers for spiritual rather than physical blessings
mark this period. This emphasis resulted from the revelation that Jesus brought that helps believers understand the
spiritual blessings that God has for those who love him.

The early Jewish Christians continued to observe the customary Jewish hours of prayer that they had grown up with

(Acts 2:1, 15; 3:1; 10:9; cf. 21:20–26). This became less prominent as Jewish believers grew to appreciate their new identity as Christians and the differences between Jewish worship and Christian worship. They often continued Jewish cultural practices for purposes of evangelism, but they withdrew from temple worship and the sacrifices because of their better position in Christ.

The early Christians characteristically assembled for prayer at times of crisis (Acts 4:24–31; 12:5). Christian leaders regarded prayer as one of their most important duties (Acts 6:5). Following the example of Jesus, Paul labored in prayer (Rom. 15:30; Col. 2:1; 4:12). Prayer was a chief feature of Christian worship, as it had been in Jewish worship (Acts 2:42; 1 Tim 2:1–8). The power of prayer to effect objective change also stands out in this period (Acts 10:4; 12; 27:24).

Prayer in the Future

The Scriptures reveal what place prayer will have in the future as well as its place in the past and present. They indicate that a time of terrible trouble is coming on the world in the future (Dan. 9:27; Rev. 6:1–19:10). Then Jesus Christ will return to the earth and establish his kingdom, which will continue forever (Rev. 19:11–22:5).

In the future, the number of believers will be quite small initially, but they will ask God to bring the Jews to faith in Jesus Christ (Jer. 31:18–19). They will also pray for the restoration of Israel as a nation (Ps. 8:3, 7, 19) and for the peace of Jerusalem (Isa. 63:15–64:12). They will ask God to vindicate his reputation by punishing their persecutors and by judging righteously (e.g., Ps. 74:10; 58:6–8). In answer to these prayers, the majority of the Jews will repent (Jer. 3:22–25).

Christians who have died and gone into the Lord's presence will offer praise and thanksgiving to God and the
Lamb, Jesus Christ, in prayer (Rev. 4:10–11). Every created thing will join them (Rev. 5:9–10, 12; 7:11–12). This
company will include martyrs who die because of future
persecutions (Rev. 7:10; 15:3–4). They will ask God to
avenge them, and he will eventually grant their request
(Rev. 6:9–10; 8:5; 19:2).

Prayers will also ascend to God from earth after Jesus
Christ returns. People will praise God for his blessings,
which will be abundant then (Isa. 26:1–19). Pagans will
confess the futility of their idols (Jer. 16:19–20) and will
turn to God in repentance and worship (Jer. 50:5; Zech.
14:16–17; Mal. 1:11). People will apparently offer prayer
in a temple in Jerusalem (e.g., Jer. 33:11; Ezek. 40:39; 46:3).
Answers to prayer will come quickly (Isa. 30:19).

Eventually every knee will bow before God in worship
(Isa. 45:23; Phil. 2:10–11). Throughout eternity people in
God's presence will communicate with him. Prayers of
praise and thanksgiving, if not petition, will characterize
life in heaven. Yet the Scriptures do not reveal the details
of our existence there.

Summary

In concluding this part of our study of prayer, let us note
some of the more important comparisons and contrasts
between prayer in the Old and New Testaments. In the Old
Testament it was chiefly the Jews who prayed to the true
God, whereas in the New Testament both groups prayed on
the same basis and with the same freedom. The basis of
prayer in the Old Testament was the person and promises
of God as God revealed them to the prophets. In the New
Testament the basis of prayer is the person and promises of

God revealed in and by Jesus Christ, which supplemented but did not contradict previous revelation.

In the early history of mankind, God spoke audibly, but as time passed, he spoke less directly. Today he rarely if ever speaks to people audibly. He has already said everything essential that he has to say, and it stands recorded in the Scriptures. Early in history people possessed little revelation of God and needed a direct word from him. Today there is much revelation of God in Scripture and, therefore, direct revelations are not as necessary as they use to be. Intelligent praying, like intelligent conversation, depends on knowledge of the person addressed. As God revealed himself through time, people's prayers became increasingly personal because they knew God better. When modern prayers are superficial, that superficiality reflects on the person praying. In earlier times, relatively superficial prayers were the only kind possible.

Whether in the Old Testament or in the New, prayers always required a mediator. Humans had to have a divinely appointed intercessor through whom they could approach God. In the early history of the race, the mediator was the head of the family and, in some instances, the Angel of Yahweh. In Israel, the mediators were the spiritual leaders, the priests and the prophets. In the present age and in the future, the sole mediator is Jesus Christ (1 Tim. 2:5).

Exodus 32:9–14

"I have seen these people," the LORD said to Moses, "and they are a stiff-necked people. Now leave me alone so that my anger may burn against them and that I may destroy them. Then I will make you into a great nation."

But Moses sought the favor of the LORD his God. "O LORD," he said, "why should your anger burn against your people, whom you brought out of Egypt with great power and a mighty hand? Why should the Egyptians say, 'It was with evil intent that he brought them out, to kill them in the mountains and to wipe them off the face of the earth'? Turn from your fierce anger; relent and do not bring disaster on your people. Remember your servants Abraham, Isaac and Israel, to whom you swore by your own self: 'I will make your descendants as numerous as the stars in the sky and I will give your descendants all this land I promised them, and it will be their inheritance forever.'"

Then the LORD relented and did not bring on his people the disaster he had threatened.

6

Theological Problems in the Prayer Life

A few years ago a young man dropped by my office for a visit. He said he had been feeling guilty because he was not spending much time praying. What disturbed him even more was that he no longer felt a need to pray. I asked him why he felt that way. He replied that he had come to believe that whatever God wanted to happen would happen. So he had concluded that praying was futile. He had stopped praying. However, as he read his Bible he could not escape the conclusion that he should pray.

This is only one of many problems that the biblical revelation about prayer creates in the minds of many people. In this chapter and the next one, I want to examine some of these difficulties.

People who reject the Bible as God's inspired revelation frequently discount prayer completely. If one does not believe that God exists, he or she will probably have few problems with prayer. Atheists and agnostics often reject prayer as outmoded superstition.

139

People have questioned the validity of prayer as early as Job's time. That patriarch referred to a skeptic as saying, "What profit should we have if we pray to the Almighty?" (Job 21:15). In our day, the question of God's existence has largely disappeared. A new question has replaced it. What difference does faith in God make? Whether God exists or not is irrelevant. It doesn't matter if you believe in God or not. He does not make his presence known, so we can ignore him if he is there, which he probably is not.

To such a person prayer appears to be self-delusion. The whole idea that there is a God and he responds to prayer by making objective changes is more than the faith of many moderns can bear. Yet the testimony of the Bible is unquestionably that there is a God, and he hears and answers prayer. Believing in prayer ultimately becomes a matter of faith, not a leap-in-the-dark type of faith, but trust or lack of trust in historical documents. Is the Bible what it claims to be, namely, the product of humans whom God's Spirit inspired to record accurately what he wanted us to know, or not? The only way to answer that question is to read the Bible with an open mind.

What I have written in this book rests on belief that the Bible is what it claims to be (2 Tim. 3:16; 2 Pet. 1:21). It reveals that there is a God and that time and space make sense if we view them in the light of what God has said. The question of whether prayer is valid can be answered by reading and believing the Bible. We will proceed on the basis that it is valid and that the Bible is not self-contradictory.

It seems that there are two types of problems that people who believe the Bible have with what it reveals about prayer. First, some of what it says about prayer seems to contradict other truths that it reveals. How can we reconcile the teaching about prayer with other revelation that seems to contradict it? This question focuses on the theological tensions of which prayer is a part. The answer to this question will be the focus of the present chapter. The second question is, "Why doesn't God answer my prayers?" This question approaches our difficulties with prayer, not from the scriptural standpoint but from the practical. Answering this question will be our concern in the next chapter.

Prayer is human speech about human concerns directed to God. It therefore involves human beings, God, and the course of events past, present, and future. To group the difficult revelations of Scripture that affect the doctrine of prayer I will divide them into problems involving people, God, and events.

What the Bible Says about Humanity and Prayer

The biblical revelation regarding the nature of human beings apparently conflicts with the biblical revelation about prayer in two particulars.

Prayer and Human Sinfulness

The Bible clearly teaches that humans are sinful and God is holy (Rom. 3:23; Isa. 6:3). How then can sinful human beings have any contact with, much less any influence on, a holy God through prayer?

The biblical resolution of this dilemma is clear and wonderful. Sinful people can approach a holy God and influence him only because God himself has made it possible for us to do so. It is possible to have such a high view of God that we conclude he is unapproachable. Indeed, this is why some people, even Christians, do not pray much. They feel that they are totally unworthy. The good news of the gospel is that, although we are totally unworthy, God has opened the way into his presence and invites us to have fellowship with himself. We can come into his presence on the basis of his Son's merit, not on our own merit. Even more amazing, he has revealed that he allows us to influence him through what we say to him. More incredible still, he has said that he will do things in response to our prayers that he would not do if we failed to pray (James 4:2).

It is possible for people to approach God because he has made it possible through Christ and has ordained it. He has taken the initiative with humankind by creating us and by reaching out to us to offer a relationship with himself through faith in his Son (John 3:16). If we will only believe his promises to us, we can enjoy an intimate relationship with the God of creation as his children. God took the initiative in providing a temporary covering for human sins, the sacrificial system, until he provided a permanent solution to our problem by sending us his Son. God encourages his human creatures to come to him and to talk to him (cf. Heb. 10:19–25). It is possible for sinful people to influence a holy God because God established prayer with that in mind. He has chosen to take people as his junior partners in running the world (2 Cor. 5:20). We participate in that partnership through prayer as well as through evangelism and by executing his will in the world.

Intercession and Human Freedom

The Bible reveals that God has created humans with enough freedom so that they are personally responsible for their decisions. Evidence of this is that when Adam and Eve chose to sin, they began to die (Gen. 2:17). When people choose to accept God's gift of eternal life in Jesus Christ, they begin to live (John 1:12; 3:36; 6:47). A few extreme Calvinists take the doctrine of election so far that they remove any personal responsibility from people. However, the great majority of Bible scholars believe that the Scriptures teach that people are responsible for their decisions and their actions. The Bible is full of illustrations of people who made choices that determined their destinies. The Pharaoh of the exodus and Moses are two classic examples.

Jesus said that all whom the Father has given him will come to him (John 6:37). God has chosen some people for salvation and not others (Eph. 1:4–5). The offer of salvation is, Whosoever will may come (Rom. 10:13; Rev. 22:17). But only the elect will come (Rom. 9:15–16). Therefore it is useless to pray for the salvation of the nonelect and to evangelize them. Yet because we do not know who the nonelect are, and because Jesus commanded us to herald the gospel to every creature (Matt. 28:19), we should pray for and evangelize everyone.

Praying for the salvation of the nonelect will not result in their coming to salvation. Therefore it is self-deceiving to "claim" the salvation of any one unsaved person. Only God knows whether that person will become a Christian. But what about praying for the salvation of the elect? What effect does our praying have on them?

If people have enough freedom to choose their own destinies, how can interceding for the salvation of the elect make any difference? If God responded to our prayer and put some sort of pressure on that individual so that he or she trusted in Jesus Christ, would he not be violating their freedom of choice?

The answer to this antinomy seems to be that prayer does not result in the subversion of anyone's will. Intercession does not result in God's coercing people. What it does do is free the person prayed for from distractions and confusions that would keep him or her from faith in Christ. In other words, intercessory prayer for the salvation of another person results in God's making it easier for that one to trust him. Whether he or she will come to faith depends on their choice, from the human perspective, and God's choice, from the divine perspective.

Recently I presented the gospel to a man in prison. I used a Four Spiritual Laws booklet to explain the gospel to him. But he spoke very little English, so I gave him the booklet in Spanish and asked him to read it out loud while I followed in my English copy. He read through the gospel presentation and continued to read the prayer expressing trust in Jesus Christ. When he finished, I asked him if he meant what he had prayed. He said that he did. This man was so ready to trust Jesus Christ that he virtually led himself to the Lord! How can we explain that kind of response? I believe that God had been working in this man's heart to convict him of his sin and to convince him of his need for a Savior. When he heard the gospel, he saw Jesus Christ as God's provision for his need.

This man was one of God's elect. Yet he had to decide to trust Jesus Christ as his Savior. The countless prayers for the salvation of God's elect that preceded his hearing the gospel were what God used to remove the barriers to his trusting the Lord. Anyone who has done much evangelism knows what a difference prayer makes in preparing the soil of people's hearts to receive the gospel message.

This is one example of a person changing his mind because of intercessory prayer. It is a worst-case scenario in the sense that choosing to trust Christ as Savior and Lord is the most difficult decision anyone can make. It is difficult because Satan resists it with all his might. The same thing happens whenever we intercede with God for others, however. The parent who prays for his child to make a wise decision sets the same forces in motion. God responds by freeing the person prayed for from unnecessary complications that would block his doing God's will. The child is still responsible for his decision, and he will not inevitably make the correct one, but he will be more likely to make the right choice. Prayer does not force or coerce another person's will. It frees it from the warping influences that hold it in bondage and inclines it to faith.

What the Bible Says about God and Prayer

The biblical revelation about God also creates problems for some people when we think about prayer. God's love, his immutability, and his omniscience confuse us.

The Love of God and Petitions

If God really loves us as much as the Bible claims, why do we have to ask him for what we need and want? Shouldn't he give us these things without our having to ask for them? If we really trusted him, would we not wait to receive whatever he chose to give us rather than asking him? Prayer seems to be an expression of weak faith rather than strong faith.

God does indeed give countless good gifts to people, even those who do not believe in him and reject him (Matt. 5:45). Yet he has commanded his children to ask for what we need (Luke 11:9). Why? Certainly it is not because God needs reminding. Neither is it because we know what we need better than he does. It is because by asking we express our dependence on him, and by expressing it we remind ourselves that we are dependent on him. Being dependent on God is not an unrealistic condition that God wants us to believe is true. It is a very real condition that we, because of our sinfulness, forget naturally and deliberately. Our proper relationship to God is extremely important for us to remember to function properly in the world. Satan got his bad start when he chose to make himself equal with God rather than remaining dependent on God. So did Adam and Eve. One of the most important things that praying teaches us is that we are dependent on God. The Christian who senses his or her dependence on God will pray, but the one who does not will neglect prayer. God commands us to ask him for what we need (Matt. 6:11–13; Luke 11:9–10).

But what about that troublesome verse that says God will not give us some things unless we ask him for them (James 4:2)? This certainly sounds as though God is holding out on us. Does that not put his love for us in question?

When I was a boy, I rode a small two-wheel bicycle for what seemed to me to be too long. All my friends were riding adult-size models, but I was still riding my small bike. One day I spotted a big bike that looked just right to me. I made sure my dad knew that that was the one I wanted. With Christmas approaching, I became very creative in the ways I brought this bike to his attention. We just happened to pass it in the store now and then. Pictures of it turned up around the house, even on his dinner plate! He knew that was the one I wanted, and he knew how much I wanted it. Sure enough, after waiting much longer than I thought was reasonable, one day there it was in the back yard. He had bought it for me.

It seems to me that God probably responds to us in a similar way. Why doesn't he give us what we need and what he wants us to have without our asking? One reason may be that he wants us to see that he is the one who has provided our needs so that we will be appropriately grateful to him. Another may be that asking and waiting builds interest in us so that when he finally does provide we will never forget his goodness. Friends of ours waited years for their first child. They prayed and prayed. When God finally gave them a baby, there were no more grateful and happy parents than they were.

But what about the baby that never comes? What about God not giving us what we request? Is this not an indication of his lack of love? Many people conclude that when God does not give them what they want and have prayed for, often for years, he does not love them. However, this is the wrong conclusion. The measure of God's love is not the number of gifts he gives us. The measure of his love is his commitment to give us only what is best for us (Luke 11:11–12). How can the denial of a baby be good for a couple? I cannot answer that, but I believe it is God's best for some couples.

Mary and I have been married for more than thirty years. We have no children. For years we prayed that God would give us children, but he never did. Mainly through reading the Scriptures we became convinced that God's withholding this gift from us was no indication that he did not love us. We discovered so many other blessings that he had given us that we could not complain about lacking children. As the years have passed, we have seen how being childless has given us opportunities for ministry that we would not have had with children. For us not having children has been a blessing, although we love children dearly and have helped to rear several. We should never measure God's love by his gifts. Whenever we question God's love for us, we need to return to Calvary. Calvary is proof positive that he loves us infinitely.

God's Immutability and Asking

Another aspect of God's character that raises questions about prayer is his immutability. The Bible says that God does not change (1 Sam. 15:29; Heb. 13:8). If that is so, then what good does it do to ask him to change someone or some situation?

The Bible teaches that God does not change in his essence, his character, and his ultimate purposes. He is always essentially what he is, a triune spirit being. Furthermore, he is consistently loving, truthful, righteous, holy. He is not good sometimes and bad sometimes. Unlike human beings, he is consistent. Moreover, what he has purposed he will perform. He will be faithful to his promises. The attribute of immutability describes God in these respects. It does not mean that he is inflexible.

The Bible also says that God changes some of his intended actions as he responds to some of our prayers (Exod. 32:14). We will discuss how and why God changes some things in answer to prayer later in this chapter. The important thing here is that we properly define immutability. If God were completely inflexible, we would live in a fatalistic world. In that case there would be no point in praying about anything because everything would be fixed. That is a pagan concept of God, not a biblical concept. It is a view of life that some Christians unfortunately have adopted.

Why would God invite us to pray if he did not respond to our prayers? What about the instances of intercession in which the biblical text says that the Lord took a different course of action because someone prayed? Surely these passages present a God who responds to the prayers of his people. He is not playing games with us when he asks us, even commands us, to pray. While God remains the same, he may change specific situations in answer to prayers without compromising his immutability.

Divine Omniscience and Prayer

The doctrine of God's omniscience has discouraged many people from praying. If God knows everything, is it not unnecessary, even foolish, to inform him of things in prayer?

Clearly God does know everything, everything possible as well as everything actual (Ps. 34:15; 139; Zeph. 1:12).

This includes, of course, the needs of all people (Matt. 6:32). It is equally clear that God wants us to petition him concerning our needs (Matt. 6:11; 7:7; Phil. 4:6–7). Obviously God does not require that we pray to inform him of things about which he is ignorant. He must have a different reason.

Parents often know much more about what their children are involved in than the children suspect. Still, most parents want their children to tell them what is happening in their lives. As they talk about their activities and interests, the parents enter into the lives of their children in a way that is impossible if there is no communication. They begin to share life together as a family. Communication is essential to fellowship.

Women are generally better communicators than men. Men tend to bottle up their feelings whereas women tend to be more free in sharing them with one another. This may be one reason women generally show more interest in prayer than men. They are more willing to open up and share what is going on inside themselves.

Sharing life together is one of God's purposes for prayer as well. It is not to inform the omniscient God but to enter into fellowship with him. This fact should affect our praying. Do we treat God as an ignorant dolt who doesn't know as much as we do, or do we enter into prayer as we would converse with someone with superior knowledge? Obviously how we think of God will affect how we pray to him.

What the Bible Says about God's Control of Human Events

Theologians use the term *divine decree* to refer to the plan that God has conceived and is executing in time and space. The Scriptures indicate that God has foreordained whatsoever happens (Rom. 8:29; Eph. 1:11). What place can prayer possibly have in such a plan?

The problem that revelation about God's foreordaining everything that happens creates concerning prayer is this. If God has foreordained whatsoever comes to pass, isn't praying useless? For example, will a farmer's prayers for rain make any difference? Will prayers for the recovery of a sick friend or loved one accomplish anything? What about a husband and wife who each pray that opposing political candidates will win an election?

In view of the clear revelation that God is in control of everything in his universe and is moving events to his intended goals, some people have concluded that the only effect prayer can have is on the person praying. We may feel better about having prayed about a particular situation, they say, but we do not alter God's will. Yet the testimony of Scripture is that God changed his mind in response to some intercessory prayers and took a different course of action than he had intended (Exod. 32:14).

The solution seems to be that prayer is a part of the plan that God has employed for accomplishing his will in history. Certain things will not happen unless people request them (James 4:2). Therefore, rather than being totally useless, prayer is a vital part of God's plan whereby he accomplishes his will. However, as a father, God will not always grant the requests of his children. But how does prayer fit into God's scheme of things?

Some of God's foreordained acts are unalterable, and no prayer can divert him from executing them (Deut. 3:23–25; Isa. 16:12; Heb. 6:6). For example, God told Jeremiah that he could stop praying for his people since their sinning had made divine discipline inescapable (Jer. 7:16; 11:14; 14:11). God revealed the time that the Messiah would appear on the earth (Dan. 9:24–26). Nothing that anyone could do, including praying, could change what God had foreordained.

However, prayer does affect the timing of some of God's foreordained acts. Moses prayed that God would be patient with the Israelites and not judge them for their sins (Exod. 32:11–13). As a result of Moses' intercession, God changed his mind and postponed judgment (Exod. 32:14). Apparently the timing of some of God's foreordained actions is not completely fixed (Jer. 18:7–10). God has built enough flexibility into his plan so in some circumstances he can take a course of action different from what he said he intended and still fulfill his purpose. Prayer can hasten blessing in some cases as well as postpone judgment (Isa. 62:6–7; Ezek. 36:37).

Sometimes Mary will call me at work and ask me to pick up a half gallon of milk on the way home. When she does that, I decide to take a different route home than I usually travel. The alternate route takes me by the dairy store. I still arrive home; I accomplish my objective. However, my plan has enough flexibility in it so I can take a different route in response to the request of someone else. Similarly, within the foreordained plan of God there is enough flexibility for God to respond to many of the requests of his people. The prayers of his people and his response, of course, are also part of his foreordained plan. They do not take God by surprise. They may take us by surprise, but they do not surprise God.

Some scholars prefer to explain the references to God changing his mind as anthropomorphisms. That is, they are descriptions of God in human terms. This explanation does not satisfy me because it still leaves the crucial question unanswered. In what sense did God change? If he did not really change in some way, the biblical writer has deceived us by describing him as changing as we do when we change our minds.

The revelation about God changing his mind helps us to appreciate again that God has designed his plan to include people as his partners in executing his will (cf. Matt. 28:19–20). He maintains control, but he gives us the privilege of working together with God to accomplish his will in the world (1 Cor. 3:9). The purpose of prayer is not to get God to serve us, but to become partners with God in bringing his will to pass in the world. *Why* God would give us this privilege is the real mystery, not *how* God does it.

The farmer who prays for rain may get rain or he may not get rain depending on how sending rain on him fits into the overall scheme of God's will. For the same reason, the person who prays for the recovery of a sick friend may or may not receive his or her desired answer. We do not know the will of God in these particulars of life. Therefore it is important that in matters like this we present our requests subject to God's will, as Jesus did in Gethsemane (Luke 22:42).

However, we can be more certain about the outcome of our praying if God has revealed his will. For example, it is futile to pray that Jesus Christ will not return to the earth, because God has guaranteed that he will return someday (Acts. 1:11; Rev. 22:20). Nevertheless it is perfectly proper to pray that his return may be soon since we do not know when he will return (Rev. 22:20). The time of his return may depend on any number of factors including our praying (2 Pet. 3:9).

In summary, there are no real conflicts between what God has revealed about prayer and what he has revealed on other subjects. We may not be able to comprehend fully how these doctrines fit together, but it is possible to see how they may.

John 14:13–14

"And I will do whatever you ask in my name, so that the Son may bring glory to the Father. You may ask me for anything in my name, and I will do it."

John 15:16

"You did not choose me, but I chose you and appointed you to go and bear fruit—fruit that will last. Then the Father will give you whatever you ask in my name."

John 16:23

"In that day you will no longer ask me anything. I tell you the truth, my Father will give you whatever you ask in my name."

7

Practical Problems in the Prayer Life

There are several theological problems connected with the doctrine of prayer, but the practical problems boil down to just one: the problem of unanswered prayer. Why does God grant some requests and not others? Sometimes it seems that God shuts out our prayers, that the heavens are brass (Deut. 28:23; Lam. 3:8). Many people share Job's frustration of crying to God day and night but receiving no reply (Job 31:35). The purpose of this chapter is to investigate the reasons for unanswered prayer and to clarify the scriptural conditions for receiving answers to prayer.

It may be helpful to examine this problem from two perspectives—the human and the divine. From the human viewpoint it is fairly easy to uncover many reasons God may not answer prayers. Some of these reasons involve improper attitudes and others spring from improper actions.

Improper Attitudes

A person may harbor improper attitudes toward prayer that paralyze his or her prayer life. Some of these attitudes prevent us from praying at all. Some people do not pray because they think prayer accomplishes nothing. If prayer accomplished nothing, people would have abandoned the practice long ago. The testimony of Scripture is that prayer does produce change, both subjectively in the person praying and objectively in the persons and situations we pray about (Num. 14:11–19; James 5:17–18).

Some people admit that prayer changes things, but they feel it is not necessary to pray except in times of extreme distress. They prefer to rely on experience (Josh. 7:2), human advice (Josh. 7:3), or personal judgment (Josh. 7:4) rather than seeking help from God. Unless our only recourse is God, why pray (2 Chron. 16:12; Isa. 30:1–2)? Prayer is the last resort for this person. Such an individual never fully realizes the possibilities of prayer. When he concludes that prayer is unnecessary, he underestimates his need for God's help (John 15:5). Conversely, when a person becomes aware of his helplessness, he will seek God's face diligently. One of our greatest needs is a realistic understanding of our deep need of God in every situation. Such an understanding drives a person to pray.

Lack of faith that God will hear prayer also hinders praying (Heb. 10:22). The kind of faith required for effective praying is belief that God *can* do what the person praying asks him to do. It is not faith that he *will* do it unless he has promised that he will in his Word. Since God is sovereign and free, we can never be sure that God will do a specific thing in answer to prayer unless he has already promised to do it. Nevertheless we can and must believe that he can do it if it is his will (Heb. 11:6). If a person does not believe this, he or she will probably not pray in the first place.

Other attitudes also limit the effectiveness of prayer. One of the most common of these is that prayer is a lever that we can use to force God to do whatever we want him to do—as if we could persuade God to serve us. This attitude often becomes obvious in what we pray and how we pray. The biblical promises to answer prayer are not trump cards that God has given us in the game of life. Since praying is talking with God, prayer contains no power greater than what words can bring to bear on our loving heavenly Father.

This faulty attitude may assume that God does not want to give good gifts to his children, and, therefore, we must coerce or trap him into doing so through prayer. Really, God is more willing to give us gifts than we are to receive them (Luke 11:9–13). The task of prayer is not to overcome God's reluctance but to lay hold of his willingness.

Another incorrect attitude toward prayer is that it can be a substitute for obedience to God. It is sometimes easier to pray than it is to obey. When we substitute prayer for obedience, prayer does not accomplish much (Josh. 7:10–12). The kind of prayer we need to pray then is a prayer of confession (1 John 1:6–9).

The idea that answers to prayer are a reward for obedience also is connected with this error (Lev. 26:3–4, 9, 18–19). Although it is true that God normally grants the requests of his *abiding* children, we should not view answers to prayer as prizes that God gives for obedience to his will. Nor does he say that he will never grant the requests of the disobedient. Whether God will grant a person's request depends on the free choice of the believer's sovereign and loving heavenly Father. People's obedience or disobedience may influence God's answer, but human obedience and disobedience are not the only factors that determine it.

Some people believe that prayer is the only thing that is necessary to meet certain needs. They believe that after a person has presented his or her petition to God that person should do nothing more to influence the situation. He or she should simply leave it in God's hands and trust him to work out his own will. This idea has led some Christians to abstain from voting, for example. They believe that praying for rulers is all that God has commanded. When we pray, they say, we should do nothing more to experience God's will. This sounds very pious, but it is an unscriptural error. In some situations, the person can do nothing to assure the granting of his request but pray. This does not mean that when we can do something we should not. Paul did not just pray for the early churches. He also wrote and visited them whenever this seemed appropriate (2 Cor. 12:21). He prayed that God would equip the Corinthian believers with all they needed to become an orderly, mature congregation (2 Cor. 13:9). However, he did not just pray to that end. He also wrote, instructed, and visited them to help them reach that goal (2 Cor. 13:10).

God sometimes even specified means that believers should use to gain the benefits we seek in prayer (Num. 21:7; James 5:14). If one asks God to do something in prayer, he should also be willing and ready to do everything within his power and God's will to bring it to pass. This includes trusting the Lord to determine the outcome. If a person is not willing to do this, he may not think that his petition is very important.

Many people believe that certain practices make prayer more powerful than it would be if they did not offer it with these practices. Four of the practices that people mistakenly think will increase the power of prayer are praying corporately, praying audibly, praying in a certain posture, and praying for a long time. Three more are praying at a certain time, praying in a certain place, and praying regularly.

Corporate praying, of course, is not wrong. People are social beings, and group praying is therefore a natural activity for us. It is a normal, divinely approved activity for people of like mind to pray together (Dan. 2:17–18; Acts 4:23–24; 12:12). The error is in thinking that there is some magical power in the prayers of a group of people who meet for prayer. This idea usually arises from a misinterpretation of Matthew 18:19–20. This passage promises God's presence when his people assemble, particularly in situations involving church discipline. It does not promise God's presence only when we assemble. God is always with his children (cf. Matt. 28:20). The dynamics of a group situation may generate new ideas and enthusiasm as people pray together. Moreover, the fact that many people have united to pray about a situation also shows God that many, rather than just a few, feel the need for what they request. Prayer meetings are a good idea, but we should not overestimate their power.

Another mistaken idea is that prayers spoken aloud are more effective than those offered silently from the heart. Scripture is clear that God hears inaudible prayers just as clearly as he hears those spoken aloud (Gen. 24:45; 1 Sam. 1:13). The God who hears prayer is the God who searches people's hearts. He does not just listen to our words (Ps. 139:23–24; Rom. 8:27). Audible praying may aid concentration and thereby make praying more effective, but it is not essentially more powerful than inaudible praying.

Praying in a certain posture, whether it be standing, kneeling, lying prostrate on the ground, or assuming any other physical position, does not in itself increase the effectiveness of a prayer. Posture alone has no special value. The position of one's body in prayer normally reflects something about his or her attitude toward himself or herself and God. It is the heart attitude that is the key to effective praying and not the physical position one may assume as he prays. However, certain postures may be more conducive to maintaining concentration in prayer.

The length of a prayer does not in itself determine its effectiveness either. As we read the prayers recorded in Scripture, we cannot help noting their brevity. The prayers of Jesus—and even his seasons of prayer—were normally short. It was apparently the earnestness and submissiveness of Jesus' prayers rather than their length that made them so powerful. His total commitment to his Father's will was undoubtedly another important factor. The Bible explicitly teaches that prayers normally should be short and not long (Eccles. 5:2). When a person multiplies his words in prayer, he also multiplies his chances for sinning with his tongue (Prov. 10:19). One must not forget that he is addressing the holy Creator of all things when he prays and that he himself is a sinful creature (Eccles. 5:2). I suspect that long prayers have bored God occasionally. God hears every prayer that we pray. Consequently we do not need to compete for his attention with long speeches (Matt. 6:7).

Neither does the time of day or night when we pray have any effect on its potency. It is impossible, for example, to prove from Scripture that an all-night prayer session is any more powerful with God than an all-day prayer session. Certain times may be more conducive to praying effectively than others, however. Likewise praying at certain inconvenient times may express one's earnestness to God.

The place where we offer prayer is not very important either. God is omnipresent and hears prayers wherever people pray. The crucial factor is not where but how we pray (John 4:20–24).

Occasionally someone will object to the practice of habitually praying at a set time of the day, for example, before breakfast. Some believers feel that this is not in keeping with the spirit of freedom that characterizes the present age. Of course, the Bible nowhere commands that Christians should pray at certain specified times, but neither does it forbid nor even discourage regular habitual praying. It may be helpful to establish a habit of regularly setting aside a portion of one's time when we can normally concentrate in prayer without distraction. The danger in doing this is that these prayer seasons may degenerate into mechanical and empty rituals devoid of any real communion with God. However, this need not happen. The important thing is reality in prayer.

These mechanical aspects of communion with God may affect proper praying, but they are minor factors in determining its effectiveness.

People can hinder the effectiveness of their praying not only by their improper attitudes *toward* prayer itself but also by their attitudes *as* they pray. There are many instances in Scripture of prayers that God did not answer because of the improper attitude of the person praying. When people forget God's instructions and promises, their prayers become less effective because God's words are his part of the divine human conversation (Jer. 2:32; 3:21; Hos. 4:6). Any conversation breaks down when one party forgets what the other party has previously said. This is also true when the words forgotten are God's words.

It is also a mistake to think that God has failed to hear our prayers because he does not respond to them immediately (Ps. 4:1). This conclusion leads to discouragement and failure to persist in prayer. God hears every prayer because he is omniscient, even though he may not respond at once.

Prayer that evidences an irreverent attitude toward God may receive only a limited response from him (Mal. 1:9).

When people lose the sense of God's uniqueness, they need a fresh revelation or reminder of him and a new dedication to him. God must occupy first place in a person's heart if he or she is to pray effectively and receive answers in return. God may not answer prayer when an idol occupies the throne of the heart (Ezek. 14:3).

A person may pray in faith believing that God can grant the request and still doubt that he will do it or do it immediately. This is true even when God has promised to do it. Someone with absolutely no faith in God is an unbeliever who has not yet learned how powerful and faithful the heavenly Father really is. God sometimes answers the prayer of the weak in faith, and when he does, the answer strengthens our faith (Judg. 6:37, 39). Weak faith paralyzes prayer, however. It is an attitude toward God that hinders effective praying (James 1:6–7).

If a person is "double minded," namely, wanting God's will some of the time but not all the time, he should not hope to receive any divine blessings including answers to his prayers (James 1:6–8). This type of person either does not pray at all, or he prays in a base way (James 4:2–10). He may not pray because to do so he would have to ask for things that presuppose a desire for God's will to happen. He really wants only what gives him personal satisfaction. If he does pray, he receives nothing from God because he asks with a base motive, a selfish desire to waste what he would receive on himself. It is no wonder that God does not grant this type of request.

Improper attitudes toward oneself in prayer as well as improper attitudes toward God can interfere with effectiveness. Selfishness is one of the major causes of unanswered prayer. Perhaps the most crass expression of selfishness in prayer is the statement of the wicked that Job voiced: "What profit should we have if we pray unto [the

Almighty]?" (Job 21:15 KJV). Prayer is often ineffective when people want only selfish matters (James 4:3). Some people come to God as spoiled children demanding that he grant them their wishes. If he does not, they sulk.

Pride, of course, is the root of selfishness. Elihu correctly observed that God does not answer prayer because of the pride of evil men (Job 35:12–13). The facet of pride that affects prayer most directly is perhaps self-confidence (Num. 14:40–45). This attitude is the antithesis of help-lessness, which is perhaps the most important attitude in prayer. Occasionally God may grant petitions that people pray in self-confidence for the glory of his Name, but this does not justify praying with a proud attitude (Judg. 20:18).

God sometimes does not respond to perfunctory prayers. These are superficial prayers that we may rattle off with-out much thought. One of the characteristics of the wicked that Jeremiah observed is that they pray in this way. God is in their speech often but far from their hearts (Jer. 12:2). Too often the children of God address their heavenly Father with the same spirit and receive the same response: no answer (Matt. 6:7).

A guilty conscience can also hinder effective praying (Heb. 10:22). The believer with sin on his conscience can-not come before God and boldly ask for things in prayer (Heb. 4:16). He needs to confess his sin first, and then God will be more open to entertain his requests (1 John 1:9).

Not only do certain attitudes toward God himself hinder effective praying, but wrong attitudes toward other people do too. Pretentiousness in prayer is one of the greatest hin-drances of this type. When a person prays so others will see and admire him, that recognition is the only answer he can expect to receive. In a sense, God has given him what he wanted because he wanted human attention more than divine attention to his prayer. Jesus Christ vigorously condemned pretentious praying (Matt. 6:5; 23:14; Mark 12:40; Luke 20:47).

An unforgiving spirit greatly limits the power of prayer (Mark 11:25). When a believer harbors a hateful attitude toward another person, he can be sure that his prayers will suffer from it (Matt. 6:14–15; Luke 9:54; 1 John 2:9–11; 4:20–21). A person who refuses to pardon another person who has committed some blunder presumes upon God's grace by which he himself has experienced forgiveness. Christians should forgive others as freely as God has forgiven us. This is the point of the parable of the two debtors in Matthew 18:21–35.

Improper Actions

Not only do improper attitudes frequently result in unanswered prayers, but improper actions often have the same result. Some of these actions have little direct connection with the practice of praying, while others determine how people offer their prayers. Some of these actions primarily concern God; others affect both God and other people. Of the activities that primarily concern God, disobedience to the divine will is the major cause of unanswered prayer. This disobedience may mean going against the Word of God by refusing to do what he directs (Deut. 1:45; Josh. 7:10–12; 1 Sam. 2:25; Jon. 1:6). It may mean failing to do all that he commands by obeying only partially. Third, it may mean going beyond God's Word by doing more than he specifies (Deut. 3:23–25).

If a person refuses to listen to the words of God, God may shut his ears to the prayers of that man or woman (Prov. 28:9). If we do not answer when God calls to us through his Word, it should not surprise us if he does not answer when we call on him in prayer (Isa. 63:15–64:12; 65:12; 66:4; Jer. 7:13–15; 11:10–12).

Idolatry is another practice that cuts the lines of communication with God. When a person makes an idol his god, his prayers may go unanswered. The idol cannot answer, and the true God probably will not answer (Jer. 2:27; 11:10; Ezek. 20:1–3, 30–31; Hos. 4:12–13). God sees that the person's hope is not in him, and he may fail to acknowledge these petitions. Let the idol answer if it can!

Advanced stages of backsliding also render prayers ineffective. In such a condition the only appropriate actions are repentance, confession, and submission to the discipline that God determines (cf. Jer. 7:16).

Refusal to confess sin in the life blocks answers to prayer (Ps. 66:18). If God's people raise sin-stained hands to him in prayer, he may hide his eyes from them (Isa. 1:15–16). It is easy to be blind to one's own sins (Isa. 58:1–9). Consequently, we should habitually ask God for forgiveness (Matt. 6:12; cf. Jer. 8:6).

The practicing of social injustice affects both God and people, and it greatly limits the effectiveness of prayer. God hears the cries of the oppressed, but he closes his ears to the prayers of oppressors whose sins separate them from God (Isa. 59:1–7). Appealing to God for personal favors when one is not willing to give his fellow man justice is hypocrisy. God will probably not grant those favors (Mic. 3:4; Mark 12:40).

In marriage, the most intimate social relationship, injustice on the husband's part in not treating his wife with the consideration due her will hinder his prayers (1 Pet. 3:7).

Several practices connected with prayer limit its effectiveness. One of these is praying with the aid of a medium (1 Sam. 28:15). Sometimes people seek help or information from God through other people either living or dead.

However, Jesus Christ is the only acceptable mediator of Christians' prayers (1 Tim. 2:5). In Israel, the prophets and priests were God's approved mediators, and God strictly prohibited any others (Deut. 18:10–11). No human mediator can give as much help in prayer as the Son of God, and to appeal to God through one only hinders effective praying. Of course, if someone addresses some other spirit being beside God, the person praying is not addressing God, and God may not answer his prayer.

Simply going through a ritual of prayer and worship without seeking God from the heart will not induce answers to prayer (Jer. 7:10; Lam. 3:41–44). Mere lip homage is not enough. For prayer to be availing, it must spring from a sincere heart in harmony with God's will (Isa. 29:13; cf. Matt. 15:8–9; Mark 7:6–7). Ritualistic praying only tells God that a person does not really feel a need to talk with him, and this attitude carries no weight with God.

There are two extremes that we should avoid regarding what we say in prayer. One is saying too much, praying too long (Prov. 10:19; Matt. 6:7–8). The other is saying too little, failing to ask for benefits that if requested we would obtain (James 4:2). One mark of a mature prayer is that it is both concise and complete. Prayer should be brief because God is great. Prayer should be comprehensive because our needs are great.

God's Viewpoint

It is helpful to understand what attitudes and actions of the person praying prevent God from answering prayer, as we have done. It is also instructive to view the problem of unanswered prayer from God's perspective to gain a fuller picture of the whole subject. Even when a person's attitudes and actions are correct, his prayers may still go unanswered. We can understand more completely why God does not always answer our prayers as we might expect because God has given special revelation that enables us to see prayer as he does.

There are some occasions when God almost never responds to prayers with a satisfying answer. If a person prays to an idol or seeks help from some unacceptable spiritual intermediary, he can be fairly sure that God will not respond to his prayers (1 Sam. 28:15). If we flagrantly disobey God's will, God normally will not respond to our prayers until we repent and confess this sin (1 Sam. 8:18; Ps. 32:3–5). There are some things that God will not grant in answer to prayer and, therefore, it is useless to pray for them (Matt. 20:20–23).

It is possible to sin to such an extent or in such a serious way that God will cease to respond to one's prayers (Num. 14:40–45; 1 Sam. 15:11, 25–26; 28:6; 2 Sam. 12:16–23). We should not think that God will always respond to our prayers if we refuse to confess and forsake our sins. The silence of God is his punishment of some who have hardened their hearts (Jer. 11:11; cf. 1 Cor. 11:30; Heb. 6:6). Even though God is very patient, his patience has a limit.

Certain situations virtually preclude God's answering prayer. Others are not so predictable. God may answer or he may not. One of the most common reasons God may not answer a prayer is that he wants to withhold response until later. The present moment may not be the best time to give the answer. The answer will come in most cases, but it may not appear as soon as we might wish it would. For example, answering some prayers involves fulfilling certain prophecies that in the will of God must wait until later (Isa. 62:6–7; Hab. 3; Rev. 22:20). Sometimes God also denied requests for further illumination of prophetic mysteries (Dan. 12:8).

God sometimes delays giving his answer to give the person praying time to reflect on his words and ways. People thereby learn a special lesson that they would not learn if God granted the request immediately (Josh. 7:6–9; Ps. 77:10–12). Some of the lessons God teaches by withholding answers to prayer are patience (Job 7:11–21), his sovereignty (Job 40:4–5), and the folly of idolatry (Jer. 11:14). God may wait to teach us to persist in our asking (Gen. 30:22; 1 Chron. 10:13–14; Isa. 62:6–7), or to pray with greater fervency (1 Sam. 1:12–16). Then when he does grant the request, we appreciate the answer more. God may delay answering to strengthen the character of the one praying or to increase his faith (Job 7:11–21; Ps. 13:5–6; 27:7–14; Mic. 7:7; Mark 5:35–43). God may also wait to allow time for a person to repent (Hos. 5:15; 7:14; Jer. 42:2–6; Joel 2:12–14). These are a few reasons God does not always answer prayers at once and why they may seem to go unanswered.

Sometimes we do not receive answers to our prayers immediately because the granting of the request takes time (Dan. 10:12–13). Demonic and satanic opposition may postpone the arrival of an answer to prayer too (cf. Dan. 9:20–23; Mark 9:28–29).

God may decline to grant a request if it is not his will. Some things are definitely not God's will for us to possess or to experience. He does not normally give these in answer to prayer (Ps. 106:15; Luke 11:11–13). However, other favors are good. These may prove to be in or out of the will of God for a certain individual when God grants them or denies them (Deut. 3:23–25; Rom. 1:13–15). God's will may allow one person to receive a certain blessing and not allow another person to receive the same blessing. The will of God is different for each person in many respects (cf. John 21:22).

God may not answer other prayers because what is needful at that moment in that situation is action rather than prayer (Exod. 14:15; Josh. 7:10).

Frequently God refuses to grant a request because he wants to do something more or better for the person than what the person praying has requested (Gen. 17:20; 1 Kings 19:4; Job 22:17; Jon. 4:8–9; 2 Cor. 12:8). It is fortunate that God did not slay every servant of his who in some moment of spiritual depression asked him to take his life! We do not always pray for what is best for us. God in his grace may not give us what is less than best.

God never forces human wills. Therefore some prayers—for the salvation of loved ones, for example—depend not only on God's conviction of the sinner, but also on the sinner's response to the gospel. Even though God wishes that all people would experience salvation, it is only those who exercise saving faith who receive eternal life (1 Tim. 2:4; Heb. 11:6; John 3:36).

In certain situations God may refuse to grant a request because he has exhausted his patience (1 Sam. 14:36–37; Isa. 49:8; 55:6–7; Jer. 11:14; 14:19–22). This is sometimes God's response to persistent sinning.

The overall principle that these particular reasons for unanswered prayer illustrate is that God does everything for his own glory. The glory of God is most important. God will always answer people's prayers when they pray for the glory of God. If he does not grant our requests, we can rejoice in the fact that his refusal to give the favors sought glorifies him more than his bestowal of them would. This is legitimate unless the refusal is due to a failure on the part of the person praying. Though God is sovereign in answering prayer, he is not arbitrary. He gives or withholds answers to prayer for his own glory and his creatures' good.

Conditions for Answered Prayer

The Scriptures clearly set forth the conditions for answered prayer. When we meet certain conditions, God will answer our prayers.

To obtain a proper perspective on this subject, we must consider the total teaching of Scripture, not just one or two verses. Occasionally we may discover a promise in the Bible that appears to guarantee unconditionally that God will answer any prayer we may offer (e.g., Matt. 7:7; John 14:14; 15:16; 16:23–24). Invariably these promises have stated or assumed conditions that become clear when we understand the whole teaching of Scripture on the subject. Every promise to answer prayer is a conditional promise.

Most of the conditions for answered prayer directly affect the person praying. The form of the words in a prayer is less important to God than the attitude of the person who prays them (Luke 18:14).

Significantly, God's promises to hear and to answer prayers are almost all to believers or for believers. God hears all prayers that people pray because he is omniscient. He even answers some of the prayers that unbelievers offer (Ps. 107:19, 28; Matt. 5:45). Nevertheless, the only prayer of an unbeliever that God promises to answer is the cry for salvation (Acts 2:21). It is only believers who are the spiritual children of God (John 1:12), and as children we have an access to our heavenly Father that unbelievers do not enjoy (Heb. 10:19–22). The many promises to answer his children's prayers constitute one of the greatest blessings God has given to those who believe on him (Matt. 7:8; 1 John 5:14–15)!

One of the most obvious conditions for receiving answers to one's prayers is that we call on God and ask him for benefits. This may seem almost too self-evident to mention, but the Bible contains many encouragements to ask God for things in prayer (Ps. 50:14–15; Matt. 7:12; Luke 11:5–13; Rom. 10:13; Phil. 4:6–7; James 1:5). We do not have many of God's blessings simply because we fail to ask him for them (James 4:2). It is so important to God that his children ask him for things in prayer that he commands us to do so (John 15:7). The first condition for receiving something from God in prayer is asking for it.

Whenever we can facilitate the reception of a gift prayed for by doing something ourselves to aid its arrival, we should do so provided that this does not involve departing from God's will (Neh. 4:9; James 5:14). Asking God to heal me, for example, and then neglecting to take my medicine is a foolish procedure. God has always worked through means more often than he has worked immediately. To abandon the means God normally uses may frustrate his granting an answer to prayer. Refusal to do all that we can to obtain our prayer request is not an evidence of great faith. Rather it proves that we either do not understand God's ways or are not serious about obtaining our requests. Of course, God sometimes answers prayer without any human means.

Helplessness is an attitude toward oneself that causes a person to cry out to God to do something that he feels incapable of doing himself. This attitude is the product of a proper understanding of the nature of God and the nature of man. This understanding can come only as God illuminates our minds concerning this truth by his Spirit. All people feel helpless occasionally, and this moves us to pray. However, as we become aware of our constant and desperate helplessness, we shall pray more and we shall pray more effectively. This attitude is an indispensable condition for effective praying (John 15:5).

A proper attitude of helplessness will evidence itself in our prayers in several ways. These characteristics are some of the conditions necessary for God to answer our prayers.

The person who feels his need greatly will not be content merely to present his petition once and then forget it. He will persist in his request as long as he thinks there is hope that God may grant it. Persistence in prayer is one of the most frequently repeated conditions for answered prayer in Scripture (Gen. 32:26–29; Exod. 17:12; 1 Sam. 23:2; 1 Kings 18:42; Isa. 62:6–7; Matt. 26:40–46). Jesus, Paul, and John taught that persistence in prayer is essential (Matt. 7:7; Luke 18:1–8; John 16:23–24; Eph. 6:18; 1 John 3:22). The child who wants a certain favor from his father will give him no rest until he gets it or learns that it is not his father's will for him to have it. This is the natural approach to our heavenly Father as well. Jesus commanded us to be persistent in our prayers (Matt. 7:7). Failure to do so will result in some unanswered prayers.

Humility is another condition for answered prayer, and it, too, is the natural product of an awareness of one's helplessness. The person praying must come before God as a suppliant, not as a dictator. Two of the Greek words for prayer mean "to beg." One word (*deomai*) is used by every New Testament writer except John and Jude. It expresses the need felt in prayer. The other word (*parakaleo*) means prayer only twice, but it means "to beg" or "to beseech" and is an admission of helplessness, lack of self-sufficiency, and utter impotency. These words reflect the humility with which we must offer prayers to avail with God.

Another characteristic of prayers that God answered in Scripture is fervency or earnestness. The person who feels his helplessness greatly cannot help praying fervently if he is serious about his request. In the Bible there are many examples of fervent prayers that God answered. We do not greatly move God to answer a prayer when we offer it half-heartedly or absent-mindedly. Obviously such a prayer is fairly unimportant to the person praying.

The helpless believer will also offer his prayers shame-lessly. Shameless praying is praying that is not afraid to acknowledge great need and to call upon God boldly to meet it (Luke 11:5–13; Heb. 4:16; 1 John 3:22; 5:14–16). The person who does not feel his need greatly may feel embarrassed telling God that he has some seemingly triv-ial need and may not pray at all. The result will be that the prayer will be unanswered and the need will remain unsatisfied.

The proper attitude toward oneself in prayer then is help-lessness. This attitude will result in certain qualities in prayer such as persistence, humility, fervency, and shame-lessness.

While a person's attitude toward himself in prayer must be helplessness, his attitude toward God must be trust or faith. Helplessness alone is not prayer. It is only frustration.

The faith necessary for God to answer prayer is not nec-essarily the confidence that he will grant the request unless he has promised that he will. It is rather the conviction that he can grant it if he chooses to do so (1 Sam. 1:18; 1 Chron. 5:20; 2 Chron. 14:11; Matt. 21:20–22; Mark 9:14–27; 11:20–25; Heb. 11:6; James 1:6–8; 5:14). We can never be sure that God *will* answer our petitions, unless he has promised to do so, since this would require a complete understanding of the whole decree of God. However, we must believe that he *can* grant them. Indeed, if we do not, we probably will not pray at all.

In addition to the attitude of faith, we must be obedient to God's will to receive answers to our prayers (Num. 21:7; Ps. 27:8; 1 John 3:22). This does not mean that we must be sinless. If that were the condition, no one could ever receive an answer from God. Being obedient means that we must be living in fellowship with God (Ps. 66:18; Mal. 3:16; 1 Tim. 2:8; 2 Tim. 2:22). This involves confessing sins when we commit them and repenting from all kinds of evil practices. One common New Testament term for living in fellowship with God is "abiding in Christ" (John 15:7 KJV).

Along with these conditions there must be sincerity in prayer. When we pray, we must pray to and for God, not to make a good impression on other people or simply because it is the time to pray (Matt. 6:6). God promises to be near those who call on him from the heart and to fulfill the desire of those that fear him (Ps. 145:18–19).

The attitude toward other people that must be behind the prayers God answers is love. The person who prays effectively should be a person who loves others as Jesus Christ loves him. This means that we must have a forgiving spirit toward others (Matt. 6:12–14; 18:21–35; Mark 11:20–25). We shall demonstrate this by praying for those who have been antagonistic toward us (Job 42:10; Matt. 5:44), by doing them good, and by treating them justly and righteously (Isa. 58:1–9). The essence of obedience to God in social relationships is the exercise of love (John 13:34–35). The person who refuses to forgive his brother refuses to love him and thereby refuses to obey God. Such a person is double-minded, doing God's will in some areas of his life and his own will in others. Such a man should not hope to receive anything, including answers to his prayers, from the Lord (James 1:7–8).

In short, the conditions for obtaining answers to prayers that concern the person praying are these. We must recognize our own helplessness and therefore pray persistently, humbly, fervently, and shamelessly. We must trust in God's ability to provide our needs, obey him by keeping his commandments, and sincerely entreat him rather than praying for human approval. We must also love our fellow men and prove this by forgiving them, praying for them, and doing them good.

There is only one condition that a prayer must fulfill to receive an answer from God. It must be in the name of Jesus Christ (John 14:12–17; 15:16; 16:23–24). The almost trite phrase *in Jesus' name* needs clarification, however. "In Jesus' name" is not the proper complimentary close to a prayer similar to "sincerely yours," which we may carelessly add at the end of a letter. When we use the phrase *in Jesus' name* thoughtlessly, it carries no special weight with God. Prayers truly prayed in Jesus' name are ones that Jesus himself could pray. They reflect his understanding of the Father, his desire for God's glory, and his submission to God's will. They are prayers prayed in view of who God is, as he has revealed himself in and through his Son. They appeal to God because of Jesus Christ's atoning work and through his mediation. In short, they are prayers that Jesus Christ could pray.

Prayers prayed in Jesus' name ask only for things within the will of God. For us to ask only those things that are God's will demands that we know the will of God in every situation about which we pray. Obviously this is impossible. Therefore, when the will of God is unknown, the way to pray in Jesus' name is to ask subject to God's will (Matt. 6:9–10; 17:19–20; Luke 22:40–44). Jesus' prayer in Gethsemane is the perfect model. He prayed that, if possible, God would remove the cup from him. If this was not the Father's will, he requested the Father's will rather than the removal of the cup (Luke 22:42). If we always sincerely included in our petitions the clause "nevertheless not my will, but yours be done," we would always receive the best answer to our prayers, but not necessarily what we requested.

Praying in God's will means praying in harmony with the promises that God has given (Exod. 32:11–14; 2 Kings 19:15–19). When we pray for God to fulfill his promises, we can have confidence that we are praying in God's will and in Jesus' name.

Prayers in the name of Jesus are also prayers for the glory of God. The purpose of prayer as well as the purpose of everything else in life is to glorify God (Col. 3:17). If a prayer does not reflect this ultimate desire, it is not a prayer offered in Jesus' name. If our ultimate desire is selfish, we may not receive an answer (James 4:3). God will always grant prayers prayed in Jesus' name because they are prayers for and subject to the will of God and for the glory of God.

Every one of God's promises to answer prayer is a conditional promise. The secret to receiving answers to prayer is asking in the proper way.

Select Annotated Bibliography

This bibliography lists a few books on prayer that the reader may want to investigate for further insight into prayer. The author consistently and frequently recommends them to others who show an interest in learning more about various aspects of prayer.

Bounds, E. M. *The Complete Works of E. M. Bounds.* Grand Rapids: Baker, 1990. Bounds has probably influenced more people to pray than any other twentieth-century writer. His many books on prayer, including this one, motivate the reader to pray more. The chapter divisions of this volume make it excellent for daily reading.

Christenson, Evelyn. *What Happens When Women Pray.* Wheaton: Scripture Press, Victor Books, 1981. Mrs. Christenson is a pastor's wife who discovered the excitement and power of prayer, and led thousands of women into that same experience through prayer seminars. The book is as helpful for men as it is for women. This is one of the best-selling books on prayer that is currently available.

Hallesby, O. *Prayer.* Minneapolis: Augsburg, 1975. This classic on prayer, often reprinted, offers many unique insights into the practice of praying. Perhaps its greatest contribution is its emphasis on human dependence that lies at the very heart of prayer. Even mature Christians have found this little book helpful to them.

Lawrence, Brother. *The Practice of the Presence of God.* Grand Rapids: Baker, 1975. This brief but powerful book illustrates from common life how to worship God amid tedious work, how to pray without ceasing. It is a great help in becoming aware of God's presence as we go through life's daily routine.

Storms, C. Samuel. *Reaching God's Ear.* Wheaton: Tyndale, 1988. The major premise of this well-written book is that people understand prayer only to the extent that they understand God. Most of the problems we have with prayer clear up when we understand God as he has revealed himself in Scripture. This is a study of God from the prayer perspective.

Strauss, Lehman. *Sense and Nonsense about Prayer.* Chicago: Moody, 1977. The author analyzes, simply and clearly, almost every practical aspect of prayer and suggests fourteen principles that should guide our understanding and practice of prayer. This is an excellent book for anyone who has questions about prayer, particularly new or untaught Christians.

White, John. *Daring to Draw Near.* Downers Grove: InterVarsity, 1977. A Christian psychiatrist uses biblical mentors—including Abraham, Jacob, Moses, David, Daniel, Hannah, Job, Paul, and Jesus—to relate prayer to the contemporary Christian. This is a creative study of some of the greatest prayer warriors in the Bible. The author makes it easy to identify with them.

Subject Index

Scripture Index